NEW BLOOD

OTHER ANTHOLOGIES AVAILABLE
FROM BLOODAXE BOOKS

for a complete catalogue of all Bloodaxe titles, please write to:
Bloodaxe Books Ltd, P.O. Box 1SN, Newcastle upon Tyne NE99 1SN.

BLOODAXE BOOKS

NEW BLOOD

EDITED BY NEIL ASTLEY

BLOODAXE BOOKS

ISBN: 1 85224 472 0

First published 1999 by
Bloodaxe Books Ltd,
P.O. Box 1SN,
Newcastle upon Tyne NE99 1SN.

Bloodaxe Books Ltd acknowledges
the financial assistance of Northern Arts.

*For Ken Smith, 'the godfather of the new poetry'
and for David Constantine, Peter Didsbury and
Helen Dunmore, the first new blood from Bloodaxe*

Cover printing by J. Thomson Colour Printers Ltd, Glasgow.

Printed in Great Britain by
Cromwell Press Ltd, Trowbridge, Wiltshire.

CONTENTS

Introduction

When I set up Bloodaxe Books over twenty years ago, I saw myself as a representative reader. I wanted to overturn Adrian Mitchell's dictum that *Most people ignore most poetry because most poetry ignores most people*, having realised that I was just one of a wide readership hungry for a much broader range of poetry; people who had been starved of the best poetry being written *because not all the best poetry was being published*.

I wanted to publish poets whose work was much appreciated by audiences at readings, and by the readers of poetry magazines, but was often not available in book form, for poetry publishing was still controlled by a small group of chaps in London, who were mostly publishing fellow southerners, Oxbridge fellows whose *verse* was read by a small coterie of academics. The poets who began to break this mould were the beneficiaries of the Butler Education Act, mostly from working-class backgrounds: the generation of Douglas Dunn, Seamus Heaney, Derek Mahon, Geoffrey Hill, Ted Hughes and Tony Harrison, outsiders from Scotland, Belfast, the Midlands and the North, whose first collections appeared in the 60s.

The growth of Bloodaxe and of several other specialist poetry publishers coincided with the emergence of a still newer generation of British and Irish poets, mostly born in the 50s and early 60s, many of them first published by these imprints. Twenty of these writers were tagged 'New Generation Poets' in a promotion organised by the Poetry Society in 1994, but this particular grouping was artificial and should not be taken as a critical guide, for it excluded some of the key figures of that generation.

The first anthologies to represent this new generation of the 80s and early 90s were both published by Bloodaxe in 1993: *The New Poetry*, edited by Michael Hulse, David Kennedy and David Morley, and Linda France's *Sixty Women Poets*, which charts the growth and flowering of poetry by women over a broader period. This generation is also strongly represented in two 1998 anthologies covering the second half of the century, *The Penguin Book of Poetry from Britain and Ireland since 1945*, edited by Simon Armitage and Robert Crawford, and Picador's *The Firebox*, edited by Sean O'Brien. The keynote of all these anthologies is pluralism: the poets are men and women from all kinds of backgrounds and cultures, from throughout Britain and Ireland as well as from overseas. They show that the subjects, voices, styles and forms of poetry are more varied now than at any time in our literary history.

When critics attack Bloodaxe, their usual complaint is that we publish 'too many books'. But Bloodaxe is the reader's publisher, offering high quality work right across the diverse range of contemporary poetry. When challenged to name people we shouldn't be publishing, one critic's *bête noire* is another's favourite writer. Everyone will find poets they like or dislike on the list, which means the list as a whole will have general support right across the board from readers and bookshops. Poetry lists which are too narrow are never sustainable. With an output of around 40 poetry books a year, Bloodaxe does the work of several publishers – all the more important at a time when other poetry lists have been cut or axed completely. If Bloodaxe didn't publish 'too many books', readers and poets would suffer.

In 1988 I edited the first Bloodaxe "house" anthology, *Poetry with an Edge*, marking Bloodaxe's first decade of poetry publishing. The second edition of 1993 was an expanded selection of work drawing on books published over 15 years by over 80 poets from Britain, Ireland, Europe, America and the Commonwealth. But it's no longer possible to represent the full range of Bloodaxe's publishing in one book: in 21 years, Bloodaxe has published over 400 titles by around 250 writers. What I felt was needed was a more focused sequel to *Poetry with an Edge*.

New Blood presents the work of nearly 40 poets who have published their first collections during the past ten years. Some of the younger poets were added to the second edition of *Poetry with an Edge*, but they belong in both books; I have, however, tried to vary their selections as much as possible. *New Blood* covers the 'New Generation' and their contemporaries, as well as the "next generation", five of whom (all born in the late 60s) took part in Bloodaxe's New Blood national promotion in 1997. To help give some sense of the shifts which have taken place even within a decade, I have presented the poets in approximate order of book publication.

I'm also aware that audiences at poetry readings find the poets' own comments about their work helpful, and with that in mind, I asked them each to write a note on the poems I selected, which I've added to my own short descriptions of their work. (In the case of Frieda Hughes, who could not write about her poems for personal reasons, I drew upon an illuminating *Observer* review of her book by John Kinsella.) In the end the poems have to speak for themselves, but I hope these comments will present you with some bearings. In selecting poems from different books and areas of work, I've tried to represent the range of each writer as much as possible within a few pages, but you would only get a full sense of each poet's particular vision by reading a whole collection of their work.

What these poets write is relevant to people's lives in some way and to their experience of the world, on an everyday as well as on a more spiritual level. This new poetry includes not just the personal but the social, political and analytical. In politics, television, newspapers and advertising, language is often negative, reductive, stripped of full expression to put across a message. Instead of being used to communicate, it is used to control thinking, as a tool of power. Our continual exposure to this manipulative, dulling force discourages openness, otherness, imagination, wonder, reaching out. *New Blood* offers fresh slants, new views and broader perspectives.

Poetry doesn't give answers as such, but it engages readers intellectually and emotionally. Readers identify with the inner debates explored by poets, with the personal conflicts explored through poetry. It also engages readers at a very basic level through its music, energy and interplay of ideas through imagery and metaphor, and through its exhilarating interrogation of language through language.

New Blood shows how today's poets can be serious and funny at the same time, and often erotic too. Their black humour can be the means of driving home a telling social or political point. In many of their poems, there's a mixture of bizarre intelligence and anarchic humour, street-cred and learning. Many of them tell stories or weave liberating fantasies. They are highly individual writers who use a wide variety of forms and styles, choosing whichever is appropriate for each poem. This new pluralism is non-conformist: there are no groups or movements, no dominant influences, with even the tetchy ghost of Larkin left to haunt an earlier generation (apart from its distortion in Stephen Knight). These new poets don't imitate but learn from their poetic models. They don't write like Plath, Bishop, Lowell, Rich, Berryman, O'Hara, Ashbery, Sharon Olds, C.K. Williams or Jorie Graham, but they would acknowledge some of these as formative influences. Mix that American experience with some formal lessons from Donne, Graves, MacNeice and Auden. Add a familiarity with Heaney, Hughes or Muldoon (plus Geoffrey Hill for some). Stir in a strong European measure, including one or other of Rilke, Lorca, Akhmatova, Mandelstam, Holub, Neruda and Brodsky. Give the Scottish poets a swig of MacDiarmid, a whiff of MacCaig, a whirl with Morgan. Throw in a wild card marked by Ken Smith or Stevie Smith, Prynne, Hopkins or Dylan Thomas. Then leave to simmer. Such an analysis holds something of their provenance – where they were bottled – but it can't capture each poet's distinctive flavour.

These poets may be voracious readers but they aren't bookish people. Unlike many writers of earlier generations, they have their feet planted firmly in the "real world". Half the poets represented in this book work as freelance writers. Although some have part-time teaching commitments, most try to make a living of sorts from readings, workshops, schools work, residencies, commissions of various kinds and literary journalism. The poet can be paid to do almost anything relating to poetry, it seems, but rarely just to write it.

Since the make-up of *New Blood* says much about Bloodaxe's publishing in recent years, here are some more statistics. This book includes 38 poets. A third are Oxbridge graduates. A third live or were born or brought up in northern England, the same proportion as for Scotland, while ten were born or grew up outside Britain. Nearly all were educated to university level, but only four teach as their main occupation. Over half have won Gregory Awards. Three-quarters of the poets are women.

A book which includes only poets from one publishing house cannot represent the whole spectrum of contemporary poetry, but an anthology from a publisher with a list as diverse as Bloodaxe's can be wider ranging than many anthologies selected from different lists by editors with narrower interests. What readers want most is to be introduced to as many different kinds of poets as possible. *Poetry with an Edge* and *New Blood* are not just birthday anthologies, they are Bloodaxe's shop-windows. My hope is that if you like the work of these poets, you will want to seek out their books.

I've not included *all* the Bloodaxe poets who've published first collections in the past ten years. Writers who've switched loyalties to other publishers aren't represented here, although we continue to publish the early work of some of them. *New Blood* represents a publishing commitment by Bloodaxe to the poets who *are* included. This should be a bonus from the reader's point of view, for unlike some editors, I've not included anyone here because I think they *should* be in the book, because other writers tell me I *ought* to include them. This "house" anthology isn't a one-off editing job, it's a house for life. I hope that says something about its special qualities as a book, that there is that strength of personal commitment behind it.

NEIL ASTLEY

John Kinsella

JAMES PENLIDIS

Selection from: *Poems 1980-1994* (1998), *The Hunt & other poems* (1998), *Visitants* (1999).

JOHN KINSELLA is the most original Australian poet of his generation. Unafraid to take on many different styles, subjects and poetic challenges, he has been unashamedly prolific. He has dusted down the pastoral, and made it a vibrant, contemporary form, especially in *The Hunt*. His *Poems 1980-1994* shows his wide range, moving from landscape and 'anti-pastorals', through to art, alternative mythologies and experimental work.

He published his first book-length collection in Australia in 1989. His latest book, *Visitants*, finds poetry in outer space, through the paranormal, cults and alien visitations. He lives in Cambridge. ●

John Kinsella writes:

I don't recognise the formalist approach to poetry – consistent syntax, clarity of meaning – or the conceptual purity of an avant-garde that denies the value of the lyric. It's the tension between form and content, rather than the smooth interaction between the two that I find interesting: a mix of styles and influences. Everything is viable subject-matter – from the commercial fetishization of the object in Warhol's factory-produced art, to wild radishes, aerials, parrots and fruit trees. 'Warhol at Wheatlands' fuses and blends popular culture with pastoral. Like 'The Rabbiters: A Pastoral', it creates an anti-pastoral, working against the bucolic idyll of the pastoral tradition. I'm always conscious of the history behind the production of a poem. In *Visitants*, I create a poetry out of obsessiveness, superstition, cultism and scepticism: poetry begins with the word, and the language itself is the subject as well as a specific object. The "alienness" exists as much in the ambiguities of the poem as it does in the 'bright cigar-shaped object', and the attempts at rational explanation of the unexplainable. 'Visitant Eclogue' is a drama between "linguistic innovation" (the alien figure) and a traditional pastoral form (the farmer). It's about breaking down and exploring boundaries. It is a landscape poem, a poem about language, popular culture, and the tensions between religion and superstition. It's also about the voice – a "song contest" in which the traditional goatherds and shepherds are replaced by a farmer and a visitant. Like all my poems, it is concerned with political, spiritual and ethical issues. I'm interested in the infinite complexity of the thing-in-itself – the word, a chilli, a plum bursting mid-flight.

Warhol at Wheatlands

He's polite looking over the polaroids
saying gee & fantastic, though always
standing close to the warm glow

of the Wonderheat as the flames
lick the self-cleansing glass.
It's winter down here & the sudden

change has left him wanting. Fog
creeps up from the gullies & toupées
the thinly pastured soil. It doesn't

remind him of America at all. But there's
a show on television about New York so
we stare silently, maybe he's asleep

behind his dark glasses? Wish Tom
& Nicole were here. He likes the laser
prints of Venice cluttering the hallway,

the sun a luminous patch trying
to break through the dank cotton air
& the security film on the windows.

Deadlocks & hardened glass make him feel
comfortable, though being locked inside
with Winchester rifles has him tinfoiling

his bedroom – he asks one of us but we're
getting ready for seeding & can't spare a moment.
Ringnecked parrots sit in the fruit trees

& he asks if they're famous. But he
doesn't talk much (really). Asked about Marilyn
he shuffles uncomfortably – outside, in the

spaces between parrots & fruit trees
the stubble rots & the day fails
                to sparkle.

Plumburst
(for Wendy)

The neat greens of Monument Hill
roll into sea, over the rise the soft rain
of plumfall deceives us in its groundburst.
If lightning strikes from the ground up,
and Heaven is but an irritation that prompts
its angry spark, then plums are born
dishevelled on the ground and rise
towards perfection...

Out of the range of rising plums
we mark the territory of the garden,
testing caprock with Judas trees,
pacing out melon runs. Behind us a block
of flats hums into dusk and the sun
bursts a plum mid-flight.

Archetypal Chillies

Are etched deep within
the human psyche – burning
seedcases bursting and re-locating
their ornamental hue. I open my
skull to your inquisitive gaze –
look, here are my chillies,
red and foreboding, hungry
for the light. See, you've done
me a favour – chillies breed on lies
but thrive on truth. They like it
both ways. Ah, if only
you'd admit to chillies – then,
then you'd understand me. The rhetoric
would flower superbly and I'd sing.
Christ, I'd sing. And you'd hear me
no matter where you hid. Your dreams
would be coloured by my song. Of chillies

and their involvement with the growth
of our souls. Of chillies and their
need for nurturing. Of the bitterness
they harvest from rejection. For this
is their strength – they are of you and I,
they are the sun's subtle rays
grown both cold and hot, they
like it both ways.

The Rabbiters: A Pastoral
(for Douglas)

That the Theocritan pick-up has been versed
in country things seems obvious, the velour
on the dashboard crazy with fresh air
rushing through the doorless cabin, the cursed
skies blackened by night. Though a moon lurks
somewhere and the spotlight cutting through
the burn-back of summer detects the jerks
of nerves and tissue – the rabbits out to chew
the burnt prongs of stubble, the halogen's
conflagration filling the omni-screens
within their eyeballs – the crack and whine
of a triple two mocks its rituals, a sign
of fading influence in a field where gravity
is a neck chop and the poem is framed by levity.

Wild Radishes

Across the dark fields the family is spread
While overhead the sky is haunted,
In the dull light they scour the crop
Never looking up as the day seems to stop.
Wild radishes missed will destroy the yield –
Bills to be paid, deals to be sealed.
But the plover's refusal to lift and drop,

And the absence of crow and parrot talk,
And the immense racket as stalk rubs on stalk,
Registers somewhere deep in the soul.
And as the sun begins to uncoil –
The deep green of the wheat uneasy with light –
The golden flowers of wild radishes bite
Just before they are ripped from the soil.

Pig Melons

As children we dashed
their brains out,
the insipid flesh
drying like chunks of pork
over the yellowing paddocks;
this murder bringing
further ruin to arable lands,
choking the native flora
with spilt thoughts
encoded as seeds
that bided their time
spitefully
until the rains
washed away the tracks
of our games, our conflicts,
percolating beneath the surface,
throwing ropes
that crept out,
securing the meagre
fertility of the place
with their rituals
of bondage.

The Fall

In the flatlands
children make empires
out of lone trees
or an aerial rising
high above the house –
a lightning strike
stretched to remove the kinks
and set as a totem
to the static of isolation.
They'd always called
him a wild boy
with his unkempt
shock of red hair;
a fireball crashing
through the atmosphere
from a forbidden perch
up high, a plunge
by which an onlooker
would only have made
the darkest of wishes.

A Bright Cigar-Shaped Object Hovers
Over Mount Pleasant

It starts in the park near Brentwood Primary School
and moves rapidly towards Mount Pleasant
a bright cigar-shaped object that darts
and jolts across the demarcation lines
of class that aren't supposed to exist in Australia
but do because even Labor voters prefer
to be on the Mount Pleasant side of the divide
if for no other reason than it pushes property
prices up. It follows the line of my escape-
route from school, the same route a man
without a face in a dark car crawls along,

calling to me as I break into a run,
the car door opening and a clawed hand
reaching out to drag me in, the cigar-
shaped object stopped stock still
and hovering like the sun, hovering
as if it's always been in that spot, always
been overhead, as hot as hell despite
the cold setting in, the sweat emanating
from my forehead, the light bright in my eyes.

Visitant Eclogue

FARMER

Well, I said to the missus that something pretty odd
was happening out here, this being the third night
lights have appeared over the Needlings; and she
said stay clear Ben Rollins, stay clear, don't go
sticking your nose into something you don't understand.
And I said, well it's my place and if anything weird
is up I wanna know about it. And it's just starting
to dry off in these parts, and it's almost a fire risk.
The everlastings will be out soon and they'll dry
until they crinkle like cellophane in the hot
easterlies, and like a blowtorch they'd go up
taking the surrounding paddocks with them.
So here I am, touched by your presence, not quite
sure what to make of it but knowing that this
is as big as it gets, that death'll have nothing on it.

VISITANT

radiant inner heart countertracking epicycloidal
windrows and approaching harvest, as if to probe your body
like a contagion that'll never let you go,
corporate body politic, engraving crops
and stooking heretics, this our usufruct,
wickerman serving up the meek & generic
as vegetation names itself and the corpse

fills with a late shower, nomadic
emergent anticipation, toxic cloud of otherness
presence before authentic essay in defence
of time's minor fluctuations,
and we comprehend your gender,
missus as signifier to your gravelled utterance

FARMER

Now keep my missus out of it, she doesn't want
a bar of it – I've already made this clear. Hereabouts
it's mainly grain, though those offerings dotting the fields
in this brooding light are sheep that'll work in trails
down to the dam and struggle for shade or shelter beneath
a single tree. Around here used to be stands of mallee
and York Gum, though I'm not sure what the natives
call it. Yep, they were here before us,
though there's none around now so I can't help you there.

VISITANT

in family structure, as dialect wears out
and you claim ownership – down from the ship
we name and conquer, that's what you'd have us think,
to go your way and validate; scarifiers and hayrakes,
all aftermath and seed drilled to be ellipsed by grains
of superphosphate, expressionist and minimal
all at once, expanding tongues as if a place of worship
might spontaneously erupt, the face of a prophet
frowning in local stone, or grinning out of a piece
of imported fruit – the simplest is most exotic

FARMER

We've always been churchgoers, and I'm proud to say
that I'm an alderman; we've just got new bells
and they ring out through the valley like they're
of another world, and believe it or not, the congregation
has almost doubled in the last few weeks. I say
it's the bells but my wife reckons it's in the air,
that people feel depleted and need something
to absorb the emptiness. When pushed, she can't put
a finger on it. The minister has mentioned it in his sermons.

Pauline Stainer

BILL TURNER

Selection from: *The Honeycomb* (1989), *Sighting the Slave Ship* (1992), *The Ice-Pilot Speaks* (1994), *The Wound-dresser's Dream* (1996), *Parable Island* (1999).

PAULINE STAINER is a latter-day English mystic who draws from an eclectic mixture of sources in myth and religion, art and science, history and landscape. According to Anne Stevenson, she writes 'sacred poetry for the scientific 21st century...wisdom and faith are still the provinces are careful, crystalline language'. Stainer herself speaks of her 'visceral Muse', while John Burnside has called her a poet 'working at the margins of the sacred', conveying sensations 'with an economy of means that is breathtaking ...her poems are not merely artefacts, they have an organic life of their own'. In her most recent poems, she evokes the spareness and luminosity of the land and seascapes of the Orkneys. ●

Pauline Stainer writes:

My writing is full of journeys made and unmade, physical and spiritual. I have always been drawn to luminous horizons; to the possibility of Keats sleeping under the Southern Cross, or the ice-pilot steering his ship through seriously old ice. 'The Wound-dresser's Dream' and 'The Ice-Pilot Speaks' sprang like sirens from journeys never made. Keats' passing reference to becoming a ship's surgeon on an East Indiaman was the scarlet particle which allowed me to explore, through the medium of dream, the look of the wound.

I want to catch in my poetry the electricity of unease: those contrary shivers when cloudshadows skim a windblown flax field, sailors sighting a slave-ship while taking Mass, death as a vivifying goddess who flutter-tongues the dying after Chernobyl. Such moments are *crossings* between conscious and unconscious, as when Leonardo injects molten wax into an ox's brain to probe 'the ventricle of memory'; or the great cats at London Zoo cross their frozen moat into the public enclosure. With the Orkney poems, I made the journey to the salt edge of things and lived there. Like Keats after reading *Lear*, I hear the sound of the sea constantly. Oddly, the authority of the light makes writing harder. The word is winnowed in the spindrift. On days of extraordinary clarity I can see Fair Isle on the horizon, austere, ravishing. In the blue wind, arctic skuas pick the eyes from a live lamb. But it is still there, the mysterious pressure of the sacred – the little foxes looking out from the Five Wounds, and the impulse to make a wholeness, a hallowing out of that. Even that.

The Honeycomb

They had made love early in the high bed,
Not knowing the honeycomb stretched
Between lath and plaster of the outer wall.

For a century
The bees had wintered there,
Prisoning sugar in the virgin wax.

At times of transition,
Spring and autumn,
Their vibration swelled the room.

Laying his hand against the plaster
In the May sunrise,
He felt the faint frequency of their arousal,

Nor winters later, burning the beeswax candle,
Could he forget his tremulous first loving
Into the humming dawn.

Sighting the Slave Ship

We came to unexpected latitudes –
sighted the slave ship
during divine service
on deck.

In earlier dog-days
we had made landfall
between forests of sandalwood,
taken on salt, falcons and sulphur.

What haunted us later
was not the cool dispensing
of sacrament
in the burnished doldrums

but something more exotic –
that sense
of a slight shift of cargo
while becalmed.

Sarcophagus

Today
in that cold yellow pause
before the rape fluoresces,
I saw the blue glow
of plutonium

men in masks and boiler-suits
on the roof
of the sarcophagus
running, running
with divining-rods in their hands

nimble as matadors,
the sun catching
the sellotape at their ankles,
the speech of birds
graphite against the sky

the oracular dove
nesting
in the reactor.

Xochiquetzal

The firefighters of Chernobyl
lie naked
on sloping beds
in sterile rooms,
without eyelashes
or salivary glands

o death
take them lightly
as the Colombian goddess
who makes love
to young warriors
on the battlefield

holding a butterfly
between her lips.

The Wound-dresser's Dream

In May 1819, John Keats considered signing on as a ship's surgeon.

I

The sirens are those journeys
we never make,
compulsory territories
fabulous as blood,

the dog-star rising
over the cobalt mines,
shafts of flywheels
inflecting the engine-room.

What drums
on the sun's image
is the art
of the unlooked for,

swans dyed russet
by heavy metals,
wax figurines
under the embalming-wound,

that chance cargo
of boat people
in sacrificial dress
for the scenting of icebergs.

II

Do you not hear the sea?

I read *Lear* in the ship's pharmacy.
The crew pray
and clean their weapons,
birds rise like grapeshot
into the Egyptian blue,

the ship ghosting
the Sargasso,
only a mizzen raised
above the ambergris
and floating weed.

We sleep lightly
as falconers,
our cargo of quicksilver
soughing against
the sun,

no dew, no dew,
only incidental bleeding.
On the 6th.
the large white pig
executed on a curved ocean,

the baffled air
full of wild ginger,
the masts dropping
medicinal gums
into the sirocco.

Such investiture
of salt
I cough my proper blood
and digest nothing
but milk.

III

In the sail-maker's loft
we watched the great moon-moths
mate on the folded sails

compound insatiate ghosts
secreting syrups
against the glisten of salt.

Above, the shrouds belling,
and ashore, the sound of
heavy firing in the hills,

the wounded with their faces
covered in little squares
of mosquito-netting

IV

We anchor off the ice-plinth.
Is there no language
to localise pain?

We bleed the source,
sense the frazil-ice
through the hull

the scream of the ermine
frozen by its tongue
to the trapper's salt-lick

the sacred conversation
of sleighs shod with runners
of jawbone

the bluish foxes
that search
through a mountain of shoes

the silver-backed jackals.

V

In the room
off the Spanish steps
the tiny rattle
of salt through sea-lavender,
the sound of nuns
in habits blue as chicory
singing the sevenfold *Amen*.

Sweetwater rises
through the shingle,
the land-wind
green with pollen,
Xenophon's men still lying
honeyed
under the toxic rhododendron.

Heavy artillery
moves into the marsh samphires.
Without morphine
the medical orderly
at the battle of Grodek
cannot fit the look of wounds
into any imaginable world.

The white clinic falls silent
round the pure chromolithography
of a lung

In the wound-dresser's dream
the eyes of the beloved
are washed with milk.

Bleaklow

They nearly made it –
the thirteen men
in the Superfortress.

The engines still crouch there
like animals
of the four directions.

We came up from the Roman road,
saw the sun
graze the fuselage

head the dead sough
through cylinder heads
they probably never saw the ground

and we lay there
like lovers
the earth not moving.

The Seals

There they were
at a solemn distance
like apostles

wedged
on white sand
in their skulking purples

the sea slung with weed
yet holding more light
than anything else.

Shaping spirits –
for when they had gone
we stood in the undertow

as if their music
were still perceived
through the skin.

Deborah Randall

IAN GROUND

Selection from: *The Sin Eater* (1989) and *White Eyes, Dark Ages* (1993).

DEBORAH RANDALL has produced two contrasting books of poems, mostly dramatic monologues celebrating the contradictions of head and heart. Sylvia Kantaris called her work 'earthed, gutsy, fiery and sensual in its dealings with the basics of life and death …a deft and womanly art', while Carol Ann Duffy liked her 'distinctive, sexy bravado'. In *White Eyes, Dark Ages*, she explores the life and mind of John Ruskin, focussing on the disparities between his emotional petrification and his deeply felt responses to art, between his sexual impotence and the fact that his most significant relationships were with women. ●

Deborah Randall writes:

Once upon a time there was sex and death. If you're having sex you can't be dead. The expression "having sex" is an abomination of our time. Nevertheless, twin fascinations. Sex, essentially a procreative act, has become estranged from its own purpose these days. Strangers can and do "have sex" and give nothing back to life or each other. Death on the other hand is truly sexy. Death is a kiss, a promise; none of us witholds our virginity from this all-consuming lover. We can't manage it, market it, exploit it.

Giving birth twice led me to Ruskin (as in 'The Blue Dome', 'Haymakers' and 'His Favourite Seat'). Cerebrally so fertile, alternately appalled by the fecundity around him and obsessed with the budding Rose. He let his yearning wife slip away to make her love and babies elsewhere. Ruskin perhaps wanted the rose to die in bud. Flowers thrilled and threatened him and he is this paradox of sex and death. To me Ruskin is sexy. He was born old and it's all happening without him. But his head is another planet, mysterious and full of wizardry. He finds the deep peace that is being not doing. Sex has to end sometime. Neither a rock nor a woman can be dissected for their soul. Water can fall upwards.

It is the artistry of man to attempt to capture and control. It is the art of women and rocks to cradle mankind but also keep their secrets. I like that restraint. Ruskin reserved himself and so should we.

Nightwatchman

Brother nightwatchman I have shared your way,
Black upon black footfall upon the crazily paved street
And eyes and hands full of each other so drunk
The wine to vinegar as we walk without talk on my tongue
And hands feeling for ourselves as only strangers can,

The lock and the alien roof and the fumble for them
Unseemly unhomely things that we build about ourselves
After marriages have broken I still dream of eggs bitter
And raw such as my father slid down his throat at dawn,
Falling from my fingers so much rage still to come,

I don't remember a time in two years when alcohol
Wasn't wailing in my veins, a substitute for tears
Like the grab and grind with a new nightwatchman,
The surprising angle of the apple in your throat
The lotion in your skin, you don't smell like him,

Stairs are unholy alliances, every one and many
Sneaking under the soles of our feet the squeak
Of female philandering as I size the nightwatchman's shoulders
Estimate the blades in there and how they shall
Rub for pleasure under my hands two wishbones wondering,

The door is the single hymen I have to admit you
And you ahead owning me and my womb without name
Flicking your beautiful hair gold and white and shampoo
And I live alone, lone as the furthest star that cannot
Be seen, little girl frantically signalling,

Nightwatchman on my carpet you are so naked, and proud
As a pose, I have watched this maleness, I see in the dark
And I know, and I'm tired, tired of the drumskin belly
The random muscle below, a perilous house of cards
Is building in me, my history frail and impersonal,

The neon snakes of your arms nightwatchman
Wind and wind about me and the carpet rolls us up
And the solitary bed is empty our flesh on the floor
In choreography, and a neighbour rapping his fifty-year-old
Indignation, an accompaniment to my game,

I open my four lips for your fingertips and my cunt weeps
As my face won't, and like an angry sponge absorbs you,
All, and when you are sleeping I watch the night,
Small boys sleep off their pleasure, I watch
The night, and wonder at such perfect death.

Ballygrand Widow

So, you have gone my erstwhile glad boy,
Whose body, I remember, stained my big cream bed,
And didn't we mix the day and the night in our play,
We never got up for a week.

If I must set my alarm again,
And feed the hungry hens in the yard,
And draw the milk from my cow on time,
And skulk my shame down Ballygrand Street
To get a drink,
It'll not be for you I think,
But my next husband,
A fine cock he shall be.

So, you are no more in this town
My lovely schoolboy, and how the floss
Of your chin tickled me.
And you swam your hands all over,
You shouted for joy, the first time.
Ah, my darling!

I wear your mother's spit on my shoes,
The black crow priest has been to beat me.
But you gave me a belly full, the best,
And they shan't take it.
The days are unkind after you, they are empty.
I lie in the sheets, the very same sheets;
You smelled sweeter than meadow hay.
My beautiful boy you have killed me.

The Blue Dome

'It is better to conceive the sky as a blue dome than a dark cavity.'
— JOHN RUSKIN

Summer is happening above the heads of the dead.
Her face is a raw daisy now
And the loom that is life has closed like the woven maypole.

Under her face, worms worming friendship,
Neighbour and neighbour mingle their benign bones,
Passing the time of day as they did aloft.
And summer if you are kind you shall forget me,
Smother her with a cypress tree which bears the load,
Hang the evening with bubbles from a blackbird.

In her coffin she hears the unnatural heat
Break into rain or the drumming feet of children
Playing over her pain.

Only then did she want air again
And water to burst on her skin pulping the parchment
Returning the spring to its source.

And summer if you are kind you shall disown
The black cavity behind the blue dome,
Summer if you are kind.

Haymakers

I'm growing my beard from the turret room
And very soon I'll climb down to youth and freedom
And cut me from the wizard who waits with wisdom
Peddling it in portions that can't restore potency.

So summer wasn't kind and didn't last forever
But it burns today and the gangers are about the fields
Embracing their light burdens
Like swatches of women in parody of the dance.

It's time to get everything in, lads to their loose lasses
Before the cannon in the sky fires a warning
And everything is over, the grains of sun snuffed out
As a smith would smother a red hot shoe in water.

One of the gangers a woman with a straight back
And every last thread of her hair up
How her demeanour mesmerises me
Because she slaves free, because she has no idea
That her labour becomes her.

His Favourite Seat

This rock-hewn seat in a favourite corner
Joins me at the hip,
And I sit and sit with it
Watching water fall
Until I can no longer tell
If I live.

The animated world goes on without me,
The mineral hours have closed my mind,
Heart still searching out its blood
And shunting round the hours,
Though clocks, even clocks,
Grow still and thoughtful.

This is a vigil of sorts,
To grow such a natural granite disguise
That it becomes me and I become the rock
With received wisdom,
To be a rock is to want for nothing,
No desire to save the world, myself,
Or even take another breath.
Not breathing, just sitting.

Marion Lomax

ROBIN COTTRELL

Selection from: *Raiding the
Borders* (1996).

MARION LOMAX grew up in Northumberland
but has lived in the South for many years.
Many of the poems of her first book, *The
Peepshow Girl* (1989), are dramatic mono-
logues and portraits, but in *Raiding the
Borders* (1996) she explores her own internal
geography, finding – as Louis MacNeice
wrote – that 'the north begins inside'. As in
Anglo-Saxon poetry, exile, separation and
grief sharpen her sense of the loss of home,
family and love, but memory offers comfort,
and by revisiting scenes and times of disloc-
ation, she repossesses the heartland from
which she takes her emotional bearings. ●

Marion Lomax writes:

I always think of Northumberland as unique – neither fully in
England nor Scotland, yet part of both because, at one time, old
Northumbria stretched as far as the Firth of Forth. Subject to
barter from the eleventh to the thirteenth century, it alternated
between Scotland and England as the border was moved. This is
the background to 'Kith' (native land), a poem about my instinc-
tive, ambivalent feelings towards our present border. It celebrates
with gratitude – and an awareness of the uneasiness of the relation-
ship over the years – a long affinity with Scotland.

I sometimes adopt a persona in my poems – usually someone
trying to survive in a difficult situation – like the wife whose hus-
band is fighting in the Gulf War ('Gulf'), or like Gruoch. She had
a better claim to the throne than Macbeth and, in marrying her
either when she was already pregnant with Lulach, her son by her
first partner, Gillecomgain, or soon after Lulach's birth, Macbeth
proves himself to be a bit of a "new man". Gruoch shared a long,
successful reign with him. Unlike Shakespeare's, this Lady Macbeth
does not go mad or kill herself. She outlives her husband to stand
defiantly on her own, a woman still capable of desire. It is Macbeth's
imagined impotence which is the real tragedy here.

These poems are concerned with divisions (emotional, physical,
sexual and social). The greatest physical and emotional division we
all experience is probably the loss of those we love through death,
and both 'Amor Diving' and 'July' are part of a sequence written
after the sudden death of my mother. I believe that – like so many
apparent divisions – even death is not an absolute barrier.

Kith

On the other side of the border
they call this *Scozia Irredenta*:
unredeemed.
        A few coffers of coins
didn't change hands; a battle was lost
instead of won; the in-between land
stays in-between.
        A line on a map
moved back through the years
            down to the Tees.
England was never an only child
but has grown to think so. Stone streets dip –
rise. They're burning coal on morning fires
in dark front rooms: smoke gusts over roofs.
Gardens, late coming into flower,
brazen it out with bright aubrietia.

I've followed the hills to Carter Bar
past lost peels, and moors where soaking sheep
stagger between tufts of died-back grass.
Standing in the rain, she's there – harassed,
hurt – a foster-mother, telling me
she hasn't much to offer. I'll take
my chance: I don't believe her.
                The bends
on the border
        won't make up their minds.
Five times
        they twist me round, but I still
head north.

Gruoch

I have a name of my own. Gruoch –
a low growl of desire. He'd say it
and crush me against his throat. Gruoch –
his huge hands stroking my hip-length hair,
grasping it in his fists, drawing it taut
either side of my arms in ropes,
staked like a tent. He'd gasp when
folds slipped open, succulent
as split stems, to welcome him in.
How I held him, squeezed the sorrow
of no son out of him – for Lulach
was only mine, fruit of first union –
of Gillecomgain, forgotten by time.

He brought me Duncan as a trophy,
sweet revenge for my father's slaughter.
Upstarts never prosper. I was the true
King's daughter, Gruoch – uttered in wonder.
Seventeen years we reigned together through
keen seasons of hunger, feasting one to other.
War nor wantons wrenched him from me:
Gruoch – a whisper, sustaining fire.

He died before the battle with Malcolm:
obsequies cradled in a dry bed.
My mouth meandered down his body –
but it was winter, no bud stirring.
Gruoch – despairing: our death rattle.

Gulf

When I wake alone in a drone of planes
it's twenty to five – three nights since you left,
just noise in the sky over someone's roof
as they tried to sleep. These pass, heading east,
their high whine muffled by thousands of feet.

I've dreamt of men, whose minds are drifting sand,
guiding you to airstrips on unknown ground.
In the glare of my lamp dust swirls and gleams,
sticks in my throat as I reach for a drink.
Tomorrow news will flash on TV screens
and, in the moment I'm not looking, you'll
be seen – acting as normal, as if all
this could be over soon – but then my glass
hits the table; it echoes round the room.

Amor Diving
(for my mother)

After the police left, having told me of your death,
I picked up the mail I'd thrown on the table
when I came in. Your card slipped out to be read:
but it's not the words you sent me from Lisbon,
the hopes for a smoother voyage after Morocco,
or even your faithful promise to meet me
which stay most strongly – for I remember
the care you would take to choose each picture,
so that was where I first looked for an answer.

I thought the name on the boat you'd picked, bobbing
in the harbour, was *Amor Diving* – just as ours did
into difficult waters – though it always surfaced.
Later, before I sang them at your service,
I realised the words were *Amor Divino*.
For all our differences, that stubborn thread
I tugged at times and frayed, holds still and strengthens
with every passing day. You are proving to me
that no one will ever love me better, telling me
what neither of us ever managed to say.

July

Watching a different sea
to the one on which you died,
I try locking a curious gull
eye to eye.

I am with him on the roof's edge,
thinking only 'high water'.
Then, 'This time last year
I had a mother.'

It's as if one grief breeds others.
When we reached the cliff path
they'd just found the body.

After you died I felt nowhere was safe
but this familiar place
could have been the exception.

Last night I dreamt you met
the murdered girl, were
trying to comfort her.

It's reassuring to think
you'll go on doing
what you were good at –

but here we are road-blocked,
our walks policed or televised,
the streets subdued, until
our late-night neighbour
starts his 4 a.m. toccata –

and when I sleep again
you have your arm around her,
and you're saying, 'I know,
I had a daughter...'

Imtiaz Dharker

IMTIAZ DHARKER's cultural experience spans three countries. Born in Pakistan, she grew up in Glasgow and now lives in India. It is from this life of transitions that she draws her themes: childhood, exile, journeying, home and religious strife. In *Purdah* (1989), she is a traveller between cultures, while in *Postcards from god* she imagines an anguished god surveying a world stricken by fundamentalism. Alan Ross in *London Magazine* admired her 'strong, concerned, economical poetry, in which political activity, homesickness, urban violence, religious anomalies, are raised' – in tightly wrought "free verse" remarkable for its supple rhythmical control. ●

Selection from: *Postcards from god* (1997: from books first published in India in 1989 & 1994).

Imtiaz Dharker writes:

The image of purdah for me was on the dangerous edge of being almost seductive: the hidden body, the highlighted eyes, the suggestion of forbidden places. But of course it is also one of the instruments of power used to bring women to heel in the name of religion.

God has been hijacked by power-brokers to justify all kinds of acts of violence. The speaker in the first 'Postcards from god' poem is a somewhat bewildered god.

This god looks out at a fractured landscape: Bombay, where I live, is a city of grandiose dreams and structures held together with sellotape and string ('Living Space'). In the face of impending collapse, the eggs in the wire basket seemed impossibly optimistic.

Sectarian violence (such as Bombay has known) suddenly forces people who had not thought of themselves as religious to take a stand, define themselves in terms of the religion they were born into, confine themselves within smaller borderlines. There is a moment when the neighbours' children become the sinister enemy, and the name of god takes on a dangerous sound.

I enjoy the benefits of being an outcast in most societies I know. I don't want to have to define myself in terms of location or religion. In a world that seems to be splitting itself into narrower national and religious groups, sects, castes, subcastes, we can go on excluding others until we come down to a minority of one.

Purdah (I)

One day they said
she was old enough to learn some shame.
She found it came quite naturally.

Purdah is a kind of safety.
The body finds a place to hide.
The cloth fans out against the skin
much like the earth that falls
on coffins after they put the dead men in.

People she has known
stand up, sit down as they have always done.
But they make different angles
in the light, their eyes aslant,
a little sly.

She half-remembers things
from someone else's life,
perhaps from yours, or mine –
carefully carrying what we do not own:
between the thighs, a sense of sin.

We sit still, letting the cloth grow
a little closer to our skin.
A light filters inward
through our bodies' walls.
Voices speak inside us,
echoing in the spaces we have just left.

She stands outside herself,
sometimes in all four corners of a room.
Wherever she goes, she is always
inching past herself,
as if she were a clod of earth
and the roots as well,
scratching for a hold
between the first and second rib.

Passing constantly out of her own hands
into the corner of someone else's eyes...
while doors keep opening
inward and again
inward.

Postcards from god (I)

Yes, I do feel like a visitor,
a tourist in this world
that I once made.
I rarely talk,
except to ask the way,
distrusting my interpreters,
tired out by the babble
of what they do not say.
I walk around through battered streets,
distinctly lost,
looking for landmarks
from another, promised past.

Here, in this strange place,
in a disjointed time,
I am nothing but a space
that someone has to fill.
Images invade me.
Picture postcards overlap my empty face,
demanding to be stamped and sent.

'Dear...'

Who am I speaking to?
I think I may have misplaced the address,
but still, I feel the need
to write to you;
not so much for your sake
as for mine,

to raise these barricades
against my fear:
Postcards from god.
Proof that I was here.

Living Space

There are just not enough
straight lines. That
is the problem.
Nothing is flat
or parallel. Beams
balance crookedly on supports
thrust off the vertical.
Nails clutch at open seams.
The whole structure leans dangerously
towards the miraculous.

Into this rough frame,
someone has squeezed
a living space

and even dared to place
these eggs in a wire basket,
fragile curves of white
hung out over the dark edge
of a slanted universe,
gathering the light
into themselves,
as if they were
the bright, thin walls of faith.

Namesake

Adam, your namesake lives
in Dharavi, ten years old. He
has never faced the angels, survives
with pigs that root

outside the door,
gets up at four,
follows his mother to the hotel
where he helps her cut
the meat and vegetables, washes
it all well, watches
the cooking pots over the stove
and waits, his eyelids drooping,
while behind the wall she sells herself
as often as she can before
they have to hurry home.

He very rarely runs
shrieking with other rain-
splashed children
down the sky-paved lane.

He never turns to look at you.
He has no memory
of the Garden, paradise water
or the Tree.
But if he did, Adam, he
would not think to blame you
or even me
for the wrath that has been visited,
inexplicably, on him.

Reflected in sheets of water
at his back
stand the avenging angels
he will never see.

The Name of god

I was washing my daughter's hair.
That was when they started
pounding at the door
banging with their sticks, and swords.
Then the fire
spread across the floor.

We ran out through the back,
her hair still wet and full of soap,
past the neighbourhood boys
with hatchets, hacking
out the name of god.

And running, we too breathed the name.
But on our tongues
it did not sound the same.

It had the sound
of children whispering,
water lapping in a pot,
the still flame of an oil-lamp.

The name of god
in my mouth
had a taste I soon forgot.

I think it was the taste
of home.

Minority

I was born a foreigner.
I carried on from there
to become a foreigner everywhere
I went, even in the place
planted with my relatives,
six-foot tubers sprouting roots,
their fingers and faces pushing up
new shoots of maize and sugar cane.

All kinds of places and groups
of people who have an admirable
history would, almost certainly,
distance themselves from me.

I don't fit,
like a clumsily-translated poem;

like food cooked in milk of coconut
where you expected ghee or cream,
the unexpected aftertaste
of cardamom or neem.

There's always that point where
the language flips
into an unfamiliar taste;
where words tumble over
a cunning tripwire on the tongue;
where the frame slips,
the reception of an image
not quite tuned, ghost-outlined,
that signals, in their midst,
an alien.

And so I scratch, scratch
through the night, at this
growing scab of black on white.
Everyone has the right
to infiltrate a piece of paper.
A page doesn't fight back.
And, who knows, these lines
may scratch their way
into your head –
through all the chatter of community,
family, clattering spoons,
children being fed –
immigrate into your bed,
squat in your home,
and in a corner, eat your bread,

until, one day, you meet
the stranger sidling down your street,
realise you know the face
simplified to bone,
look into its outcast eyes
and recognise it as your own.

Geoff Hattersley

MOIRA CONWAY

Selection from: *Don't Worry* (1994) and *'On the Buses' with Dostoyevsky* (1998).

GEOFF HATTERSLEY has been a key figure in small press poetry publishing, editing *The Wide Skirt* for many years. He lives in Huddersfield, and works as a machine operator in a plastic injection moulding factory.

His poems are accessible and entertaining, but their apparent simplicity belies a shrewd intelligence as much in tune with larger events as with the daily happenings which seem to form their subject. His reading of many other poets, especially Americans like Frank O'Hara, has produced not show-off quoting, but tonal balance and sly humour, and a subtle, streetwise style in which New York meets New Yorkshire. ●

Geoff Hattersley writes:

'Frank O'Hara Five, Geoffrey Chaucer Nil' was obviously written to wind some people up, as were many of my poems. An anti-social stance is implicit in almost all of them. Well, it's hard to be satisfied with the way things are, isn't it? While it's important for me to express this, I've never wanted to be the sort of writer who carries a big stick and bludgeons the reader with it. There has to be some humour. In 'Singing' I was trying hard not to confound seriousness with solemnity. I don't like poems that have made that mistake.

'Remembering Dennis's Eyes' is based on a real incident, though the witness to the robbery was my brother, David. He was only twelve at the time, which I'm not sure the poem makes clear.

'Death's Boots' was written in 1991 while the Gulf War was happening, and that exerted an influence on it. Not that it's about the Gulf War. It's about an enigmatic character called Death's Boots. I'm not sure exactly who he is but his footprints are everywhere.

I do know exactly who 'The New Mr Barnsley Something' is, however. The poem is one of many concerning stupid and dangerous characters encountered drinking in the Barnsley and Rotherham areas. The new Mr Barnsley Something had four older brothers who were even more violent, though none of them was quite as bad as their little sister.

I read in a review that '*On the Buses* with Dostoyevsky' is about the discrepancy between serious and popular culture. I thought it was about industrial deafness, family life, and being a literary neophyte from a non-literary background. Anyway, what discrepancy?

Frank O'Hara Five, Geoffrey Chaucer Nil

I think on the whole I would rather read
Frank O'Hara than Geoffrey Chaucer, and
this fine, non-smoking morning could well be
the right time to try out a new (uh hum)

poetic form. It's the funniest thing:
I am *here*, thirty years of age, having
put booze and all sorts of, say, 'dubious
substances' behind me, now sweating it

all out in a small, constipated room
with a plump tomato of a woman,
conjugating Middle English verbs. I have
developed a line, a very brief line,

in gestures of friendliness, and in my
trousers an idea is taking shape.

Singing

Everybody's singing, they call it that.
In the bath, in the kitchen, in the car
on the way to work. And what do they sing?

They sing, Ooh Ba-by, let me feel your love.
They sing, Ooh Ba-by, need you're-las-tic-lips.
They sing, Ain't ea-sy for no man a-lone.

Everyone, in their cars, bathrooms, kitchens
– singing, singing. This is happiness, here.

Remembering Dennis's Eyes

He always blinked too much,
like an overnight guest who leaves
with the toilet paper in his holdall
or leaves a dry blanket
covering a wet bed.
Even with the balaclava
turned round to hide his face
I could see him blinking
through the makeshift eyeholes.

Gimme the bastard bag
he yelled, tugging at it.
The iron bar bounced on
the guard's helmet five times
before he fell to his knees,
another four or five before
he lost his grip on the bag.
You saw nowt, *nowt*, Dennis hissed,
pinning me to the wall
with one hand, waving the bar
like a conductor with the other.

The last time I saw him,
years later, years ago,
he'd just tried to kill his ex-wife,
had been stopped by
his ten-year-old daughter.
He was running toward Darfield
like a wind-up toy
with a pair of kitchen scissors
sticking between his shoulder-blades.

Death's Boots
(for Ian McMillan)

In a previous incarnation, I climbed mountains
and sang my own praises, anticipating the trend.

On each wall of my home hung gaudy self-portraits.
I was posing for the camera before I invented it.

Then I was told I was a fool, that my career was over
for perfecting the ever-lasting light-bulb.

So I took a post kicking the oats out of farmers.
The money was good. Death's Boots, they called me.

I became involved because I saw no reason not to.
The reasons would pile up later like wood-shavings

from the pencils of the man who wrote *The American Century*.
That man was me, Death's Boots.

The New Mr Barnsley Something

on the front page of the *Chronicle*
once promised to crack my skull
but that's beer down the urinal

and I can turn to page two
as calmly and as amused
by his pectorals as anyone else

recalling also one Saturday night
as part of a large crowd watching
Mr Barnsley Something bouncing

another man's head on a car bonnet
while shouting 'I'll teach thee
to make eyes at our lass.'

And suddenly I wonder
what became of him –
the other man,

the one they lifted
like a ticking bomb
and drove away, slowly.

On the Buses with Dostoyevsky

Because of the steelworks
that deafened my dad
our telly was always
too loud, so loud
it formed a second narrative
to what I was reading
up in my room
in my late teens – I'd have
Hemingway and *Kojak*,
Alias Smith and Jones and Poe.
All that noise! Car chases
and gunshots, sirens, screams,
horse racing and boxing,
adverts for fishfingers,
floor cleaner and fresh breath;
and Knut Hamsun starving,
Ahab chasing his whale.
I felt like a learner driver
stalled at a traffic light,
a line of lorries behind me.
Because of the steelworks
that closed in 1970
and which I never saw
except as a skeleton,
I like silence and calm,
I like silence and smoke
cigarettes in the dark.

Brendan Cleary

MOIRA CONWAY

Selection from: *The Irish Card* (1993) and *Sacrilege* (1998).

BRENDAN CLEARY is a playfully honey-tongued and self-mockingly dissolute performance poet and stand-up comic, exiled from Co. Antrim to Newcastle and Brighton: going off his head in his performance pieces, going back inside in more personal poems about rootlessness, inner exile and estrangement. The anti-poet Harry Novak calls his poems 'sad movies of Irish soul...Cleary's given up his joker for the ace of hearts. He's left the pub for the confessional, blabbering his tale of woe like a late night wag who's high on the muse and the music, tearful and brilliant like a kind of Hank Williams on acid.' ●

Brendan Cleary writes:

'Sealink' and 'Slouch' are much more obviously personal poems than the others selected here. The confessional voice is that of my own attempting to reconcile or come to terms with a long-standing inner tension with regard to my Ulster background and my life in exile in the vastly differing culture of "mainland" Britain.

In the other poems I adopt a persona, often an irreverent voice continually trying to demystify what I see as the values of the dominant ideology. I like this voice to use irony, to exhibit a mischievous deadpan humour. 'The New Rock n Roll' is a sardonic swipe at the media circus who have tried to popularise poetry purely from a point of view of surface image, to make the craft more digestible for colour supplements or middle-class coffee tables.

The label "performance poet" has stood me in good stead in terms of getting work in usual places over the years. Sometimes, I feel, it has disadvantages, as if my poems were too readily dismissible or "throwaway". I think otherwise. Inner exile. Alienation. Spoiled Idealism. There's a few clues. May I respectfully suggest you figure out the rest for yourselves.

I hope my work is accessible and entertaining. I believe poetry can be that without cheapening itself intellectually. Mind you, just because my poems can sometimes be funny doesn't mean for an instant that I'm not deadly serious...

Sealink

I've left on this dreary boat once too often
so now this return route means home.

It doesn't mean Whitehead, its sloth & inelegance
or the blood & semen stirring Belfast bars.

Nor do I look back when I walk the plank
or stare transfixed from decks at dwindling docks.

There's nothing vaguely romantic to leave behind,
just the graffiti sprawl of miserable Larne,

the ignoble funnels & towers of Ballylumford
merging with the smog as my childhood slips.

Let's face it, I came here to escape bad blood,
a land of martyrs with their kneecaps smashed,

bonfires blaring as the war drums sound,
a debris of legs scooped into bin liners

& I wanted to escape the daggers behind language,
the subtle testing out process at teenage discos.

'What school do you go to then?' meant
'Which foot do you kick with? right or left?'

How you said it, Derry or the other place
registered a sharp & knowing smile.

I settle quick, hold back a flood of playbacks,
contemplating only breakfast I gaze straight ahead,

never even wipe back the window's condensation...

Slouch

Their bar-stools have slouched them too early
though later half-cut they start to sidle up

'Hey Pat, why not fuck off where you came,
back to the bogs, shouldn't you be picking spuds?'

They have eyes with no causes, their smug voices
in drunken unison jeer & mock my voice.

Perhaps when the hangover hits I'll take them up,
return meekly, submerge myself in landscape,

more like submerge myself in Black Bush –
bury myself in selfish small-town intrigue,

or if I had any passion left for bland slogans
I could even do my bit for the 'armed struggle'.

But the echo of Lambegs burst my skull,
I've spent too long licking up to England.

I've been the brunt of their stunted comedians
I've lived in comfort but amid canned laughter

& this latest encounter could come to fisticuffs
although till now I've played the Irish card with charm.

They probe me: 'Mick, do you even belong in this country?'
I won't slouch too early so I gleefully reply

'just as much as you belong in mine'...

The New Rock n Roll

Still, there was quite a decent turn-out really,
at least 25 if you count Seamus, the organiser's dog.

Where were all those teenage girls in his sweatshirt,
his dressing-room crammed with bottles of Jim Beam?

Traces of cocaine on a dog-eared limited edition,
rumours in tabloids he'd trashed his hotel room again?

& how come even though he dresses in all that black gear,
clearly the broody type, he can't whip us up to a frenzy?

Last night there was no crazy rocking in the aisles,
we weren't reciting along with him, swaying like geese

& we never held our lighters up, grinning near the end,
when he kicked into his sonnets like anthems...

Boys' Own

Sure Jo & I used to spend hours doin' it,
tinnies in the fridge & digging sounds like,
we'd think up ridiculous Country titles.

Remember Ireland's rugby team, a cracker
*Dropkick me, Jesus, through the goalposts
of Life*. It's a pretty hard act to follow.

& Jo always said politely: *Another beer there*,
it glided down smooth like a torchlit procession
as I kept a watchful eye on his whiskey bottle.

One night we just creased, ended up in stitches
when Jo came out with *Jesus stole my girlfriend*.
OK, maybe you had to be there, know what I mean?

Chicken & Sex

Chicken & Sex. That's what I need constantly. I am quite insistent upon this but as usual she ignores me. Sometimes in the stillness, in the flakes of snow or leaves falling, sometimes it feels as if she is the one with all the problems & I am the therapist. It's costing me £20 to feel so special.

What's happening now behind her eyes? I've just been revealing to her what I truly need & crave. Chicken & Sex. She just gazes at the flakes of snow or leaves falling outside in the stillness.

Does all this therapy mean my entire childhood happened in some sort of warzone? Answers, I want them! Once she asked me what colour I would paint the world. That really stumped me. I made one up. A bright shocking yellow. Something that would distort all of our heads. Then she told me I masturbated too often. How could she have known that? She may be silent but she's wise.

One day when the flakes of snow or leaves weren't falling I arrived early, let myself into her studio. She had left me a virtually illegible note. I think it read: *Gone to see my therapist.* So she had one too, I was reassured. I noticed when she did appear she looked pale & her clothes didn't seem to fit. I know what that feels like. At that stage I had yet to mention anything at all about the Chicken & Sex. Those were happier days, less confusing. Now she tells me again over the decaffeinated coffee that I'm *getting there.* I still don't know where she means...

Maura Dooley

DAVID HUNTER

Selection from: *Explaining Magnetism* (1991) and *Kissing a Bone* (1996).

MAURA DOOLEY's poetry is remarkable for embracing both lyricism and political consciousness, for its fusion of head and heart, 'her sharp and forceful intelligence' (Helen Dunmore); but also has poise and playfulness, showing 'the possibilities of affection and humanity within a world you accept as also sinister and lonely...Her best work pares things to the essence in a lovely rueful economy of words and feeling' (Ruth Padel). Her work has 'a shrewdly historicising sense...It takes us across borders – literal, emotional and figurative – into states of mind which are entirely her own, yet instantly recognisable by all of us' (Andrew Motion). ●

Maura Dooley writes:

The advice *You should get out more* is true for me in a most particular way. I should walk more. Wordsworth knew that but his long walks weren't exceptional at a time when everyone walked more and thought less of it. The walk has left its legacy in our language: in our speech, in the rhythms of iambic pentameter. Many of these poems began to form in my head during long walks in the Pennines or shortcuts through city backstreets. There's something both invigorating and releasing about walking alone, a path you know well, in the absence of friends, family and phones: contemplation and perambulation.

'Mansize' and 'What Every Woman Should Carry' use everyday personal objects, a handkerchief and a bag, to unpack some of the ghosts of tragedy, mystery and joy folded away inside. 'Up on the Roof' and 'Does It Go Like This?' are about the cracks that craze the clear glaze of love and the need to look at them quietly, freely and alone ('Up on the Roof' owes something of its mood to the Goffin/King song). 'Heart' and 'Dancing at Oakmead Road' were written after my father's death. 'Heat' and 'History', now that I see them side by side, strike me as the before and after of a love affair, although not necessarily the same love affair...but 'History' also tries to touch on our uses of what, after the event, we understand as popular history, the first moonwalk or the fall of the Berlin Wall. 'Letters from Yorkshire' is about the bridge of friendship that links and holds together two different places and people, and that, in essence, is what I hope to do in a poem, build some stepping stones so that disconnected moments suddenly make sense.

Letters from Yorkshire

In February, digging his garden, planting potatoes,
he saw the first lapwings return and came
indoors to write to me, his knuckles singing

as they reddened in the warmth.
It's not romance, simply how things are.
You out there, in the cold, seeing the seasons

turning, me with my heartful of headlines
feeding words onto a blank screen.
Is your life more real because you dig and sow?

You wouldn't say so, breaking ice on a waterbutt,
clearing a path through snow. Still, it's you
who sends me word of that other world

pouring air and light into an envelope. So that
at night, watching the same news in different houses,
our souls tap out messages across the icy miles.

Mansize

Now you aren't here I find
myself ironing linen squares,
three by three, the way
my mother's always done,
the steel tip steaming over your
blue initial. I, who resent
the very thought of this back-breaking
ritual, preferring radiator-dried
cottons, stiff as boards, any amount
of crease and crumple to this
soothing, time-snatching, chore.

I never understood my father's trick,
his spare for emergencies, but was glad
of its airing-cupboard comforts often enough:
burying my nose in it, drying my eyes
with it, staunching my blood with it,
stuffing my mouth with it. His expedience,
my mother's weekly art, leaves me
forever flawed: rushing into newsagents
for Kleenex, rifling your pockets in the cinema,
falling on those cheap printed florals,

when what I really want is Irish linen,
shaken out for me to sink my face in,
the shape and scent of you still warm
in it, your monogram in chainstitch
at the corner. Comforter, seducer, key witness
to it all, my neatly folded talisman,
my sweet flag of surrender.

Heart
(for my father)

Your heart, like an old milk tooth
hanging by a thread: a strength we'd test
with temper, trust, the exquisite tug of truth.

Enlarged, we knew what that meant.

And now, I want your big heart here,
to chart its absences: the yellow stream
of bitterness, the silver river of malice,
the empty shore of Lake Envy,

all the landscapes it had never known
and all the different countries it contained.

History

It's only a week but already you are slipping
down the cold black chute of history. Postcards.
Phonecalls. It's like never having seen the Wall,
except in pieces on the dusty shelves of friends.

Once I queued for hours to see the moon in a box
inside a museum, so wild it should have been kept
in a zoo at least but there it was, unremarkable,
a pile of dirt some god had shaken down.

I wait for your letters now: a fleet of strange cargo
with news of changing borders, a heart's small
journeys. They're like the relics of a saint.
Opening the dry white papers is kissing a bone.

Heat

Summer swells like a fruit.
Long evenings hang
the way small insects hug a storm lantern.
Already we have forgotten about covers,
know that this will be called *that summer*.

Staring across fields to where
water breaks this land in two
we cannot see it gleaming,
even under full moon.
Intention and purpose
are hidden among long grasses,
the low coughs of sleeping beasts.

How to peel the truth from this,
expose the ripeness of the moment,
juice in our mouths and our hands still clean.

Does It Go Like This?

The day seawater swilled my lungs
he guided me back without ever once touching me.
Lying on shingle, like the two halves
of the equator, I thought my heart would burst,

not knowing in which element it drowned.
Now, two hundred miles from him, beached
on larkspur, lark song, I struggle to remember
something I used to know: *did it go like this? Like that?*

How did it start? At Capel-y-Ffin what rises
from dark red dirt, what's netted now
is flotsam of sheepskull filleted by maggots,
a dead pony's ribs taut as ships' rigging

and here, where a draught of summer
rinses tired skin with cuckoo syncopation,
with percussion of bees, old fears rush in
fierce as a tide. Blood, not birdsong

pulses at my ear: the strong cross-currents
that beat in these shallows, the meat
and bone under bright meadow grasses,
the heart's tricky business of staying alive.

Remember the day we saw divers trawl the Thames
heavy with rosaries of gas and rope,
angels with black rubber wings and serious faces
dropping through mist and into the deep, like psalms?

What is that tune whose words I try to catch
Does it go like this? Like this? How does it begin?
I dredge up only the middle, a jaded chorus,
of a song I used to know right through by heart.

Dancing at Oakmead Road

Sometimes I think of its bright cramped spaces,
the child who grew there and the one we lost,
how when we swept up for its newest lover
the empty rooms were still so full of us.

The honeyed boards I knew would yet hold close
our dusts, some silver from my father's head,
the resin of the wood would somehow catch
in patina the pattern of his tread.

That time in the back room, laughing and drunk,
Geraldo and his orchestra, a tune
that had you up and waltzing and me quiet,
my throat so achey at the sight of you,

glimpsing for a second how it might have been
before his mouth went down on yours, before
the War, before the children broke into
the dance, before the yoke of work. Before.

What Every Woman Should Carry

My mother gave me the prayer to Saint Theresa.
I added a used tube ticket, kleenex,
several Polo mints (furry), a tampon, pesetas,
a florin. Not wishing to be presumptuous,
not trusting you either, a pack of 3.
I have a pen. There is space for my guardian
angel, she has to fold her wings. Passport.
A key. Anguish, at what I said/didn't say
when once you needed/didn't need me. Anadin.
A credit card. His face the last time,
my impatience, my useless youth.
That empty sack, my heart. A box of matches.

Up on the Roof

You wonder why it is they write of it, sing of it,
till suddenly you're there, nearest you can get
to flying or jumping and you're alone, at last,
the air bright. Remembering this, I go
with my too-light jacket up to the sixth floor,
out onto the roof and I freeze under the stars
till he comes with my too-heavy jacket, heavier
and heavier, as he tries to muffle my foolishness.
A blanket on a fire (he says) and it's true
I am left black, bruised a little, smouldering.

You can sit with a book up there and reel in
life with someone else's bait. You can let your eyes
skim the river, bridges, banks, a seagull's parabola.
At night, you can watch the sky, those strange galaxies
like so many cracks in the ceiling spilling secrets
from the flat above. You can breathe. You can dream.

But he turns to me, as you'd coax a child
in the back of a stuffy car: *we could play I-Spy?*
I look at the black and blue above and the only
letter I find is 'S'. I cannot name
the dust of starlight, the pinheaded planets,
but I can join the dots to make a farming tool,
the belt of a god: all any of us needs is work,
mystery, a little time alone up on the roof.

W.N. Herbert

ALEX BLACK

Selection from: *Forked Tongue* (1994), *Cabaret McGonagall* (1994), *The Laurelude* (1998).

BILL HERBERT is a highly versatile poet who writes both in English and Scots. Born in Dundee, home of William McGonagall and *The Beano*, he writes phantasmagorical satires in which real and imagined characters wreak havoc with cherished myths. *The Guardian* described his work as 'a weird mix of Desperate Dan, MacDiarmid and Dostoyevsky'. But he can also be tenderly lyrical, offering fond homage as well as terrier wit. Exiled in recent years to Newcastle, he has committed many verse outrages against good taste, not least *The Laurelude*, in which Stan Laurel takes a leaf out of Wordsworth's *Prelude*, with hilarious results. ●

W.N. Herbert writes:

The first poem's set in Timex: it's a work-induced daze, pondering my simultaneous love of everything Italian and of fish & chips. Benni's was the ice cream shop I grew up near. I think they (the chip shops) symbolised the period just behind my childhood: before change, before destruction, before death. 'Cab Mag' is about being a loser from Dundee, just like McGonagall. He brought out people's fear and hatred of *Ahrt*, which was what the Dadaists wanted from the Cabaret Voltaire. I wanted to write something that rollicked like Dunbar. Basically it's a Weimar website for oafs and softies.

'The Baby Poem Industry' is from that period when NewGen started replicating – it was a nod to Robert that we were happier writing than changing the nappies. It's written in Unglish, a dialect derived from info-speak, ad-talk, and plagiarising Mark E. Smith.

I wrote 'The Black Wet' (rain, as opposed to snow, which is white) on moving to the Lake District and understanding precipitation for the first time. Wordsworth never mentions the continuous deluge – he was obviously receiving backhanders from the Tourist Board. So I thought a relentless catalogue of real and imaginary terms for rain might help. Sif is the wife of Thor. Huey, Dewie and Louie are the nephews of Donald Duck.

'To a Mousse' was inspired by a sludgy dessert I got served up at Moniack Mhor. This damn thing would never ever set: it was a three-inch thick wobble board; there was mousse loose aboot that hoose. Eventually the angels beat me up and pointed out this was a perfect opportunity to revisit the stanza form of Burns's 'To a Mouse'.

Praise of Italian Chip-Shops

That summer, in a small glass booth,
I sat and set strapless watches
to within ten seconds of test time
all day, as the women did all year.

Fifty a tray times twenty trays
whilst trying to chat to Joe Capitelli
whose name kept sending me into
a dreamtime of Dundee shopfronts:

'Grilli', 'Piscini', 'Vissocchi'...
an ice-cream float of mock-Italian:
'Scella da peas on da coontah...'
here was another timelessness:

red mock-leathery booths of the cafés
in Blairgowrie and the Ferry,
yellow tartan formica of the chippers
in Stobswell and Arbroath.

The decor of my time machine was fixed
on sub-Art Deco forever, binding me
to Italy, binding the fifties to me on
a waft of milk-froth and lard.

Here I first perceived the rocket
machinery of coffee-propulsion;
the catholicity of a sugar-censer;
the madonna of the knickerbocker glory.

Here I first encountered the folded
pizza supper that would translate
as *calzone* in Florence; the two tiles
in the Spanish chippie in Blackness,

painted with tambourined dancers like
some pan-European Eve and Adam: all these
cleared me an hour from the cease-
less grasping hands of the clock

in which I could just sidle in
to the black marbled cool dimness
of Benni's on the corner of Corso Street
and buy time back in sliders.

Cabaret McGonagall

Come aa ye dottilt, brain-deid lunks,
ye hibernatin cyber-punks,
gadget-gadjies, comics-geeks,
guys wi perfick rat's physiques,
fowk wi fuck-aa social skills,
fowk that winnae tak thir pills:
gin ye cannae even pley fuitball
treh thi Cabaret McGonagall.

Thi decor pits a cap oan oorie,
ut's puke-n-flock à la Tandoori;
there's a sculpture made frae canine stools,
there's a robot armadillo drools
when shown a photie o thi Pope,
and a salad spinner cerved fae dope:
gin ye cannae design a piss oan thi wall
treh thi Cabaret McGonagall.

We got: Clangers, Blimpers, gowks in mohair jimpers,
Bangers, Whimpers, cats wi stupit simpers –
Ciamar a thu, how are you, and hoozit gaun pal,
welcome to thi Cabaret Guillaume McGonagall.
We got: Dadaists, badass gits, shits wi RADA voices,
Futurists wi sutured wrists and bygets o James Joyce's –
Bienvenue, wha thi fuck are you, let's drink thi nicht away,
come oan yir own, or oan thi phone, or to thi Cabaret.

Come aa ye bards that cannae scan,
fowk too scared tae get a tan,
come aa ye anxious-chicken tykes
wi stabilisers oan yir bikes,
fowk whas mithers waash thir pants,
fowk wha drink deodorants:
fowk that think they caused thi Fall
like thi Cabaret McGonagall.

---

dottilt: daft, confused; *oorie*: dirty, tasteless; *gowks*: fools; *ciamar a thu:*
how are you (Gaelic).

Fur aa that's cheesy, static, stale,
this place gaes sae faur aff thi scale
o ony Wigwam Bam-meter
mimesis wad brak thi pentameter;
in oarder tae improve thi species' genes,
ye'll find self-oaperatin guillotines:
bring yir knittin, bring yir shawl
tae thi Cabaret McGonagall.

We got: Berkoffs, jerk-offs, noodles wi nae knickers,
Ubuists, tubes wi zits, poodles dressed as vicars –
Gutenaben Aiberdeen, wilkommen Cumbernauld,
thi dregs o Scoatlan gaither at Chez McGonagall.
We got: mimes in tights, a MacDiarmidite that'iz ainsel contradicts,
kelpies, selkies, grown men that think they're Picts –
Buonaserra Oban and Ola! tae aa Strathspey,
come in disguise jist tae despise thi haill damn Cabaret.

Panic-attack Mac is oor DJ,
thi drugs he tuke werr aa Class A,
sae noo he cannae laive thi bog;
thon ambient soond's him layin a log.
Feelin hungry? sook a plook;
thi son o Sawney Bean's oor cook:
gin consumin humans diz not appal
treh thi Bistro de McGonagall.

Waatch Paranoia Pete pit speed
intil auld Flaubert's parrot's feed,
and noo ut's squaakin oot in leids
naebody kens till uts beak bleeds
and when ut faas richt aff uts perch,
Pete gees himsel a boady search:
thi evidence is there fur all
at thi Cabaret McGonagall.

kelpies: river spirits in the shape of horses; *selkies*: seals which can take on human form; *leids*: languages.

We got: weirdos, beardos, splutniks, fools,
Culdees, bauldies, Trekkies, ghouls –
Airheids fae thi West Coast, steely knives and all,
welcome to thi Hotel Guillaume McGonagall.
We got: Imagists, bigamists, fowk dug up wi beakers,
lit.mag.eds, shit-thir-beds, and fans o thi New Seekers –
Doric loons wi Bothy tunes that ploo yir wits tae clay;
ut's open mike fur ony shite doon at thi Cabaret.

Alpha males ur no allowed
amang this outré-foutery crowd
tho gin they wear thir alphaboots
there's nane o us can keep thum oot,
and damn-aa wimmen care tae visit,
and nane o thum iver seem tae miss it:
gin you suspeck yir dick's too small
treh thi Cabaret McGonagall.

There's dum-dum boys wi wuiden heids
and Myrna Loy is snoggin Steed,
there's wan drunk wearin breeks he's peed –
naw – thon's thi Venerable Bede;
in fack thon auld scribe smells lyk ten o um,
he's no cheenged'iz habit i thi last millennium:
gin thi wits ye werr boarn wi hae stertit tae stall
treh thi Cabaret McGonagall.

We got: Loplops and robocops and Perry Comatose,
Cyclops and ZZ Top and fowk that pick thir nose –
Fare-ye-weel and cheery-bye and bonne nuit tae you all,
thi booncirs think we ought tae leave thi Club McGonagall.
But we got: Moptops and bebop bats and Krapp's Last Tapeworm
          friends,
Swap-Shop vets and neurocrats, but damn-aa sapiens –
Arrevederchi Rothesay, atque vale tae thi Tay,
Eh wish that Eh hud ne'er set eye upon this Cabaret.

Culdees: members of the Columban church; *loons*: young men; *Bothy tunes*: ballads
from Scotland's rural North-East; *ploo*: plouh; *foutery*: excessively fussy.

The Baby Poem Industry Poem
(for Robert Crawford)

Sensitive male minus labour pains equals poem.
Production rate increases in inverse proportion
to childcare units as follows:
one couplet per five cloacal nappy non-encounters;
one stanza per non-milky-upchucked-on work shirt;
one poem per missed shift of all-nite colic alert;
one volume per year of missed meals in which
beans must be halved and omelettes rolled
into yellow trumpets, plus three hours
of night-night rituals including
march round marmite-smeared dwelling
chanting 'When-uh sains' and nine renditions
of story about haddock.

Sensitive male supplies plethora of loving
metaphors for partner including:
galactic dugong, pot-noodle of robust abundance,
shining wing-mirror extension for caravans
of completed individuation process,
symphonic Fiorentina team of
graceful scheduling and loving-kindness.
Sensitive male imagines he can see
the creation of the universe
by examining her epesiotomy scars.

Sensitive male's publisher is not impressed,
rendering the sensitive one suddenly aware
of the fact
he has not had sex
for nine months.
He casually but lyrically mentions this
in evening poem faxed home from work.
Sensitive male is suddenly aware on returning home
of unusual ice-pick adorning his forehead.

Partner commences series
of highly-profitable elegies.

The Black Wet

It's raining stair-rods and chairlegs,
it's raining candelabra and microwaves,
it's raining eyesockets.
When the sun shines through the shower
it's raining the hair of Sif,
each strand of which is real gold
(carat unknown).

It's raining jellyfish,
it's raining nuts, bolts and pineal glands,
it's raining a legion of fly noyades,
it's raining marsupials and echnidae,
it's raining anoraks in profusion.
It's siling, it's spittering, it's stotting, it's teeming,
it's pouring, it's snoring, it's plaining, it's Spaining.

People look up, open their mouths momentarily,
and drown.
People look out of windows and say,
'Send it down, David.'
Australians remark, 'Huey's missing the bowl.'
Americans reply, 'Huey, Dewie and Louie
are missing the bowl.'

It is not merely raining,
it's Windering and Thirling, it's Buttering down.
It's raining lakes, it's raining grass-snakes,
it's raining Bala, Baikal, and balalaikas,
it's raining soggy sidewinders and sadder adders.
It's raining flu bugs, Toby jugs and hearth-rugs,
it's raining vanity.

The sky is one vast water-clock
and it's raining seconds, it's raining years:
already you have spent more of your life looking at the rain
that you have sleeping, cooking, shopping and making love.
It's raining fusilli and capeletti,
it's raining mariners and albatrosses,
it's raining iambic pentameters.

Let's take a rain-check:
it's raining houndstooth and pinstripe,
it's raining tweed. This is the tartan of McRain.
This is the best test of the wettest west:
it is not raining locusts – just.
Why rain pests
when you can rain driving tests?

It is raining through the holes in God's string vest.

To a Mousse

O queen o sludge, maist royal mousse,
yir minions bear ye ben thi hoose,
O quakin sheikess, lavish, loose,
                dessert o fable:
ye pit thi bumps back oan ma goose
                and shauk ma table.

Ye lang cloacal loch o choc,
grecht flabby door at which Eh knock,
and wi ma spunie seek a lock
                tae mak ye gape,
ye flattened, tockless cuckoo clock
                that drives me ape.

Come let me lift ye tae ma mooth
and pree yir pertness wi ma tooth –
ye slake ma hunger and ma drouth
                wi wan sma bite:
come pang ma toomness tae thi outh
                wi broon delight.

Let ane and aa dig in thir spades
and cerve oot chocolate esplanades,
and raise thir umber serenades
                at ilka sip:
sweet Venus, queen o cocoa glades
                and thi muddied lip!

pang: stuff; *toomness:* emptiness; *outh:* utmost.

Jackie Kay

INGRID POLLARD

Selection from: *The Adoption Papers* (1991), *Other Lovers* (1993) and *Off Colour* (1998).

JACKIE KAY's first collection, *The Adoption Papers*, tells the story – her story – of a black girl's adoption by a white Scottish couple. Her second book, *Other Lovers*, explores different kinds of love, and includes a sequence on the Blues singer Bessie Smith. In *Off Colour*, her poems treat illness, sickness and health, examining not just the sick body but the sick mind, the sick society, the sickness of racism and prejudice. Her poems are, by turns, poignant, bitter-sweet, joyous and funny; they are 'brave and honest, full of pain and rage, but also a tenderness which is not sentimental, but deeply moving' (Elizabeth Bartlett). ●

Jackie Kay writes:

A strange thing happens when you have to write or talk about your own work: it becomes like the work of somebody else and you try to think of something to say after the event. The 'event' which really matters is the writing and what you say afterwards is as false as hindsight. We are our own unreliable narrators. Take this with a pinch of salt.

I think I will always be interested in identity, how fluid it is, how people can invent themselves, how it can never be fixed or frozen. In *The Adoption Papers*, I took my own life as a subject and fictionalised it. I was adopted and brought up in Scotland. The 'Somebody Else' in the last poem here is the other person I could possibly have been. Fate is mixed up with identity. My original birth father was Nigerian: 'Pride' takes my face as a kind of a map back to the imaginary Nigeria.

I like mixing fact with fiction and trying to illuminate the border country that exists between them. Being black and Scottish, I've often been asked where I'm from. 'In my country' is a mixture of many experiences. 'Twelve Bar Bessie' was also inspired by a real incident when Bessie Smith fought off the Ku Klux Klan single-handedly. I've loved Bessie Smith's raunchy blues since I was a girl, and wrote about her in *Bessie* (Absolute Press). I like the way that jazz too is fluid. I've written a novel, *Trumpet* (Picador), about a jazz trumpeter who lives his life as a man but is discovered to be a woman after death. From blues narratives on, I've always been interested in the way music tells the story of identity.

from The Adoption Papers
Chapter 3: The Waiting Lists

The first agency we went to
didn't want us on their lists,
we didn't live close enough to a church
nor were we church-goers
(though we kept quiet about being communists).
The second told us
we weren't high enough earners.
The third liked us
but they had a five-year waiting list.
I spent six months trying not to look
at swings nor the front of supermarket trolleys,
not to think this kid I've wanted could be five.
The fourth agency was full up.
The fifth said yes but again no babies.
Just as we were going out the door
I said oh you know we don't mind the colour.
Just like that, the waiting was over.

This morning a slim manilla envelope arrives
postmarked Edinburgh: one piece of paper
I have now been able to look up your microfiche
(as this is all the records kept nowadays).
From your mother's letters, the following information:
Your mother was nineteen when she had you.
You weighed eight pounds four ounces.
She liked hockey. She worked in Aberdeen
as a waitress. She was five foot eight inches.

I thought I'd hid everything
that there wasnie wan
giveaway sign left

I put Marx Engels Lenin (no Trotsky)
in the airing cupboard – she'll no be
checking out the towels surely

All the copies of the *Daily Worker*
I shoved under the sofa
the dove of peace I took down from the loo

A poster of Paul Robeson
saying give him his passport
I took down from the kitchen

I left a bust of Burns
my detective stories
and the Complete Works of Shelley

She comes at 11.30 exactly.
I pour her coffee
from my new Hungarian set

And foolishly pray she willnae
ask its origins – honestly
this baby is going to my head.

She crosses her legs on the sofa
I fancy I hear the *Daily Workers*
rustle underneath her

Well she says, you have an interesting home
She sees my eyebrows rise.
It's different she qualifies.

Hell and I've spent all morning
trying to look ordinary
– a lovely home for the baby.

She buttons her coat all smiles
I'm thinking
I'm on the home run

But just as we get to the last post
her eye catches at the same times as mine
a red ribbon with twenty world peace badges

Clear as a hammer and sickle
on the wall.
Oh, she says are you against nuclear weapons?

To Hell with this. Baby or no baby.
Yes I says. Yes yes yes.
I'd like this baby to live in a nuclear free world.

Oh. Her eyes light up.
I'm all for peace myself she says,
and sits down for another cup of coffee.

In Jackie Kay's *The Adoption Papers* sequence, the voices of
the three speakers are distinguished typographically, including:

DAUGHTER: Palatino typeface
ADOPTIVE MOTHER: Gill typeface

In my country

walking by the waters
down where an honest river
shakes hands with the sea,
a woman passed round me
in a slow watchful circle,
as if I were a superstition;

or the worst dregs of her imagination,
so when she finally spoke
her words spliced into bars
of an old wheel. A segment of air.
Where do you come from?
'Here,' I said, 'Here. These parts.'

Twelve Bar Bessie

See that day, Lord, did you hear what happened then.
A nine o'clock shadow always chases the sun.
And in the thick heavy air came the Ku Klux Klan
To the tent where the Queen was about to sing her song.

They were going to pull the Blues Tent down.
Going to move the Queen out of the town.
Take her twelve bar beat and squash it into the ground.
She tried to get her Prop Boys together, and they got scared.

She tried to get the Prop Boys together, and they got scared.
She said Boys, Boys, get those men out of here.
But they ran away and left the Empress on her own.
She went up to the men who had masks over their head

With her hand on her hips she cursed and she hollered,
'I'll get the whole damn lot of you out of here now
If I have to. You are as good as dead.
You just pick up the sheets and run. Go on.'

That's what she done. Her voice was cast-iron.
You should have seen them. You should have seen them.
Those masks made of sheets from somebody's bed.
Those masks flying over their heads. Flapping.

They was flapping like some strange bird migrating.
Some bird that smelt danger in the air, a blue song.
And flew. Fast. Out of the small mid western town.
To the sound of black hands clapping.

And the Empress saying, 'And as for you' to the ones who did nothing.

Pride

When I looked up, the black man was there,
staring into my face,
as if he had always been there,
as if he and I went a long way back.
He looked into the dark pool of my eyes
as the train slid out of Euston.
For a long time this went on
the stranger and I looking at each other,
a look that was like something being given
from one to the other.

My whole childhood, I'm quite sure,
passed before him, the worst things
I've ever done, the biggest lies I've ever told.
And he was a little boy on a red dust road.
He stared into the dark depth of me,
and then he spoke:
'Ibo,' he said. 'Ibo, definitely.'
Our train rushed through the dark.
'You are an Ibo!' he said, thumping the table.
My coffee jumped and spilled.
Several sleeping people woke.
The night train boasted and whistled
through the English countryside,
past unwritten stops in the blackness.

'That nose is an Ibo nose.
Those teeth are Ibo teeth,' the stranger said,
his voice getting louder and louder.
I had no doubt, from the way he said it,
that Ibo noses are the best noses in the world,
that Ibo teeth are perfect pearls.
People were walking down the trembling aisle
to come and look
as the night rain babbled against the window.
There was a moment when
my whole face changed into a map,
and the stranger on the train
located even the name

of my village in Nigeria
in the lower part of my jaw.

I told him what I'd heard was my father's name.
Okafor. He told me what it meant,
something stunning,
something so apt and astonishing.
Tell me, I asked the black man on the train
who was himself transforming,
at roughly the same speed as the train,
and could have been
at any stop, my brother, my father as a young man,
or any member of my large clan,
Tell me about the Ibos.

His face had a look
I've seen on a MacLachlan, a MacDonnell, a MacLeod,
the most startling thing, pride,
a quality of being certain.
Now that I know you are an Ibo, we will eat.
He produced a spicy meat patty,
ripping it into two.
Tell me about the Ibos.
'The Ibos are small in stature
Not tall like the Yoruba or Hausa.
The Ibos are clever, reliable,
dependable, faithful, true.
The Ibos should be running Nigeria.
There would be none of this corruption.'

And what, I asked, are the Ibos faults?
I smiled my newly acquired Ibo smile,
flashed my gleaming Ibo teeth.
The train grabbed at a bend,
'Faults? No faults. Not a single one.'

'If you went back,' he said brightening,
'The whole village would come out for you.
Massive celebrations. Definitely.
Definitely,' he opened his arms wide.
'The eldest grandchild – fantastic welcome.
If the grandparents are alive.'

I saw myself arriving
the hot dust, the red road,
the trees heavy with other fruits,
the bright things, the flowers.
I saw myself watching
the old people dance towards me
dressed up for me in happy prints.
And I found my feet.
I started to dance.
I danced a dance I never knew I knew.
Words and sounds fell out of my mouth like seeds.
I astonished myself.
My grandmother was like me exactly, only darker.

When I looked up, the black man had gone.
Only my own face startled me in the dark train window.

Somebody Else

If I was not myself, I would be somebody else.
But actually I am somebody else.
I have been somebody else all my life.

It's no laughing matter going about the place
all the time being somebody else:
people mistake you; you mistake yourself.

Ian Duhig

LEON McAULEY

Selection from: *The Bradford Count* (1991), *The Mersey Gold-fish* (1995) and *Nominies* (1998).

IAN DUHIG's witty and bizarre poems are profane and profound, often drawing on tall tales and strange episodes from history, Irish legend and colonial lore, fed by obsessions ranging from inherited treachery to religion and homelessness, fish and dolphins.

'Duhig telescopes topical allusions, scholarly references and coarse humour into tightly-shaped surreal poems which burst open with explosive moral force' (Alan Brownjohn). 'Seeking out the brutalities behind the euphemisms of history, Duhig's poems express a Browningesque delight in distortion' (Patrick Crotty, *Modern Irish Poetry*). ●

Ian Duhig writes:

I began writing assiduously, if not seriously, about the time my son Owen was born in 1986. He changed everything. Amongst much else, I felt an ebb and flow between the Irish culture I inherited from my parents and the world of histories waiting on my Yorkshire-born son. In no time at all my bones had turned to coral and my eyes were pearls.

'Fundamentals' was inspired by Livingstone's diaries. 'From the Irish' is from entries in Dineen's great dictionary of Irish, while 'Margin Prayer from an Ancient Psalter' is a prequel to the Sweeney cycle of early Irish poetry. 'The First Second' refers to a Catholic folk-myth that only Jesus Christ was exactly six feet tall. 'The Egg' Konstant, who taught me at school in London, was made Bishop of Leeds about the time I wrote this.

'Untitled': little has been heard of the poet Patrick Muldoon since his abduction by aliens. 'Fred' quotes from and borrows the form of Thomas Gray's 'Cat Drowned in a Tub of Goldfishes', but a Mersey goldfish is a turd.

'Nominies' is a Yorkshire word meaning 'children's chants', its use being recorded in the Opies' book which also lends the poem its epigraph. The word itself is probably sectarian in origin, from 'In Nomine Patris' as 'Hoc est Corpus' gave us 'hocus pocus' and 'hoax'. A commission, the poem was structured something like an old pier machine, jerking through tableaux of horrible murders for a coin. The section here is roughly the last third and was written shortly after water was privatised.

Fundamentals

Brethren, I know that many of you have come here today
because your Chief has promised any non-attender
that he will stake him out, drive tent-pegs through his anus
and sell his wives and children to the Portuguese.
As far as possible, I want you to put that from your minds.
Today, I want to talk to you about the Christian God.

In many respects, our Christian God is not like your God.
His name, for example, is not also our word for rain.
Neither does it have for us the connotation 'sexual intercourse'.
And although I call Him 'holy' (we call Him 'Him', not 'It',
even though we know He is not a man and certainly not a woman)
I do not mean, as you do, that He is fat like a healthy cow.

Let me make this clear. When I say 'God is good, God is everywhere',
it is not because He is exceptionally fat. 'God loves you'
does not mean what warriors do to spear-carriers on campaign.
It means He feels for you like your mother or your father –
yes I know Chuma loved a son he bought like warriors
love spear-carriers on campaign – that's *Sin* and it comes later.

From today, I want you to remember just three simple things:
our God is different from your God, our God is better than your God
and my wife doesn't like it when you watch her go to the toilet.
Grasp them and you have grasped the fundamentals of salvation.
Baptisms start at sundown but before then, as arranged,
how to strip, clean and re-sight a bolt-action Martini-Henry.

From the Irish

According to Dineen, a Gael unsurpassed
in lexicographical enterprise, the Irish
for moon means 'the white circle in a slice
of half-boiled potato or turnip'. A star
is the mark on the forehead of a beast
and the sun is the bottom of a lake, or well.

Well, if I say to you your face
is like a slice of half-boiled turnip,
your hair is the colour of a lake's bottom
and at the centre of each of your eyes
is the mark of the beast, it is because
I want to love you properly, according to Dineen.

Margin Prayer from an Ancient Psalter

Lord I know, and I know you know I know
this is a drudge's penance. Only dull scholars
or cowherds maddened with cow-watching
will ever read *The Grey Psalter of Antrim.*
I have copied it these thirteen years
waiting for the good bits – High King of the Roads,
are there any good bits in *The Grey Psalter of Antrim?*

(Text illegible here because of teeth-marks.)

It has the magic realism of an argumentum:
it has the narrative subtlety of the Calendar of Oengus;
it has the oblique wit of the Battle-Cathach of the O'Donnells;
it grips like the colophon to The Book of Durrow;
it deconstructs like a canon-table;
it makes St Jerome's Defence of his Vulgate look racy.
I would make a gift of it to Halfdane the Sacker
that he might use it to wipe his wide Danish arse.
Better its volumes intincted our cattle-trough
and cured poor Luke, my three-legged calf,
than sour my wit and spoil my calligraphy.
Luke! White Luke! Truer beast than Ciarán's Dun Cow!
You would rattle the abbot with your soft off-beats
butting his churns and licking salt from his armpits.
Luke, they flayed you, pumiced your skin to a wafer –
such a hide as King Tadhg might die under –
for pages I colour with ox-gall yellow...

(Text illegible here because of tear-stains.)

Oh Forgiving Christ of scribes and sinners
intercede for me with the jobbing abbot!
Get me re-assigned to something pagan
with sex and perhaps gratuitous violence
which I might deplore with insular majuscule
and illustrate with Mozarabic complexity
Ad maioram gloriam Dei et Hiberniae,
and lest you think I judge the book too harshly
from pride or a precious sensibility
I have arranged for a second opinion.
Tomorrow our surveyor, Ronan the Barbarian,
will read out loud as only he can read out loud
selected passages from this which I have scored
while marking out his new church in Killaney
in earshot of that well-versed man, King Suibhne...

(Text completely illegible from this point
because of lake-water damage and otter dung.)

The First Second

My young son claimed total recall from the sperm
    last bathnight, which stopped me like a clock.
From my immobilised hands he prised the oil
    that proofs his scalp against baptism
and turned right through me his orphanmaker-look,
    locking the continents of my skull
into jigsaws of his own. Then he could see

stars round my head from that crack on the lintel
    one fathom dead above the bald rug
outside my parent's cellar, hear my father's
    'Only Christ grew six foot to the nail!'
and Father Konstant's 'Imagine a steel egg
    bigger than the entire universe
brushed once every century by a dove's wing:
    when that whole egg is worn to nothing
is as the first second of eternity!'

Untitled

> *'Out of these enmities, indeed, would come a new efflorescence*
> *– especially of poetry in the work of Seamus Heaney, Michael*
> *Longley, Derek Mahon and Patrick Muldoon.'*
>> F.S.L. LYONS,
>> Culture and Anarchy in Ireland

No Derry slubberdegullion with college airs,
no mushroom visions in Wexford sheds (well, not *Wexford*),
no continuing city father with gentle breasts
and high voice since his run-in with the barber's missus –
no: you were the quietest. You were surely the best:

Running Over Toads on the Ballygawley Roundabout;
Squeezing the Brains out of Toads – each an epiphany.
Your assurance crumbled after your quoof escaped,
excluding yourself from your own anthology
(but nearly everybody else into the bargain),

finally you lost even what you stood up in
to some imposter from a parallel universe
(the Moy). He painted spectacles over your face
in all your photographs, insinuated himself
into your fingerprints and remodelled your signature.

To this very day I remain flabbergasted
that folks could be suckered by such a flagrant hoax,
and I've a flabber not gasted by a trifle,
'Paul'! Sounds Mick to me. Now 'Patrick' from the Old Norse
Pad-rekr, at least that means something: 'Exiler of Toads'.

Fred

Not all that tempts one's wand'ring eyes
is fairly won as lawful prize,
    hinc illae lachrymae.
Fred burned his fairground booth red-gold,
my son, then I, then he were sold.
    Fred died the self-same day.

A few hours purpling our kitchen shelf...
kaput. I think he killed himself.
   I hid him from the son
I later told a dolphin stirred
to bear Fred's soul Fish-Asgardward,
   how royally he'd gone!

But no man wrote his epitaph;
with one flush of the cenotaph –
   transubstantiation.
A consummation to be wished,
Fred was the word made flesh made fish,
   Prince of Goldfish Nation.

My dreams ran red with Fred going west;
down The Cut, through Liverpool's est-
   uary (take a breath),
the Irish Sea's transgenic soup
boiling like a kaleidoscope
   half-life to life-in-death;

on to Dublin and to Galway
where swam ashore folk from Cathay,
   swore grey-eyed Columbus;
where fish circling St Brendan's Mass
bear Fred to the Americas,
   to survive in numbers.

from Nominies

> '*...to children the days of the year change at midday
> rather than midnight.*'
>
> IONA AND PETER OPIE
> The Lore and Language of Schoolchildren

I prayed to the ghost of Carrie
of the telekinetic powers,
of high school proms that go like bombs
and most traumatic showers;

I raised the shade Janet Leigh played
from her plug in the Bates Motel
and I conjured Norman's Mother
for help from Hell as well.

Silence held then crashed in a storm
while starlight gathered in a wheel;
the forest's moleskin dark was torn
by showers of stainless steel;

a fiery crown came crashing down
I thought I'd won, I roared and cheered
a goose well-cooked, but when I looked
the King had disappeared;

a drought made he, a river me,
I rumbled underneath my banks
that water's not what should be bought
but still I babbled thanks;

I crowded him, I clouded him,
I'd put an end to all his spells,
the interim I hunted him
from England's holy wells;

I worked him under Yorkshire sky
where the Red King popped his clogs
who forgot about Yorkshire drought
which rains cats and dogs.

The gold harp said 'The Red King's dead.
Long live the King! The King must die!
You're due North-West, so all the best,
but now you have to fly.

That was the house of your Nine Queens,
ten is for Gabriel Rangers;
beyond your ken we'll meet again
and won't be strangers.'

The golden harp sank in a coin
that rolled like night across my eyes
for the hour was the eleventh,
though ten made no goodbyes.

Where around me once was forest
and the great wheels of clocks,
a smell of pine surrounded me
and six walls of a box.

But I had a final angel
to break me free without a word
so from that hole my captain soul
soared upwards like a bird.

The Republic of Underland
lay below and gleamed like bone
and though children were playing there
I heard old people groan.

Tears like shillings welled in my eyes
and through their lenses I could see
Walter Calverley's, the Red King's
faces. They looked like me.

The Sun flashed like a tinsel toy
and the sky was a bell of space;
the moment boomed and dumb and doomed
I kissed her cold glass face.

The Moon flashed like a tinsel toy,
sand flowed up and down the timer;
which way is left and right and wrong
and who is John Rhymer?

It was midnight and it was noon,
the light of noon and moonlight swapped;
the music of spheres filled my ears
until the penny dropped.

Elizabeth Garrett

ALISON RICHARDS

Selection from: *The Rule of Three* (1991) and *A Two-Part Invention* (1998).

ELIZABETH GARRETT is a lyric poet in the tradition of Robert Graves whose subjects are the eternal themes of poetry: love, childhood, family, truth, time and memory, innocence and experience. The informing spirit of her poetry is music – in the cadences of the language, the forms and resolutions of the poems. Relating her "metaphysical" poetry to John Donne's, Francesco Rugnoni calls her poetry 'almost glacial in its composure, intangible and profoundly erotic'. Hers is a poetry of 'formal grace and sinewy intelligence' (Maura Dooley). 'There is a static, frozen moment quality about many of the poems' (Philip Gross). ●

Elizabeth Garrett writes:

As a teenager I was a competent springboard diver; and I can still recreate a keen internal sense, both physical and aesthetic, of the dive's trajectory: the arc, the cleavage of the water, the miraculous moment of resurfacing. There are more than metaphorical similarities, for me, between writing a good poem and doing a good dive. It's as though, in the act of writing, there has to be a passage from one element to another, and then a return to the original element – a sort of epiphanic resurfacing.

Perhaps for this reason, at readings, I often "introduce" my poetry with 'The Reprieve', without preliminary commentary: it embodies the pre-verbal structure of this movement which I think informs much of my writing: the return as epiphany. In this particular selection, it's present in the formal movement of 'Unguentarium', as in 'History Goes to Work', 'Ribes rubrum' and – almost in reverse – in 'Contrary Motion'.

The shapes of poems interest me. Even before you begin to read a poem your eye registers the poem's shape in relation to its surrounding whiteness. The crafting of this shape is not simply "packaging", but a more conscious elaboration of that fundamental form, or movement, the pre-verbal structure. I love the possibilities of rhyme and the persuasions of rhythm, and I think that music – my greatest passion – deeply informs my use of language. Just as sound emerges out of and returns to silence – and is therefore intimately connected with it – so I feel keenly my poetry's suspension in silence.

History Goes to Work

The soft-boiled egg is emptied
But makes a humpty-dumpty head
Reversed. Numbskull! Bald pate!
You know the spoon's importunate
Knock knock will wake the dead.

The silver spoon lies on its back
And spoons the room all up-
Side-down but never spills a drop:
The ovoid walls adapt their laws
And never show a crack.

The egg lies in the silver spoon
And yolkless words lie on the tongue
And all that's in the spoon-shaped room
Swears it is square; no books
Were cooked. The egg is done.

Remorse rests in its velvet drawer
Lapped in the sleep of metaphor,
The soul rests in the open palm
And will not put its shell back on,
And calmly waits for more.

Vista
(for my mother)

Standing, with your back turned, taut at work,
Wearing the day's frosted willow-grey skirt
Like a bell of smoke, while a child went on colouring
Under the spell of the Lakeland-Cumberland arc,
You turned suddenly hearing the doorbell ring.
Turned? No – *spun*, till the skirt flared its carillon
And all the poplar leaves of the world shone
Silver, their green gone in the wind's turning.

And here I am, wise at the open door
Trying to remember what it was I came for,
Struck by a knowledge of beauty years beyond
Anything I had yet come to understand,
Watching you disappear down that corridor
Of brilliant sound, my stolen breath in your hand.

The Reprieve

I was a diver then:
In every limb, the coil
And spring of a poem – heaven
Couldn't hold me. Cool
On my flaming cheeks, the air
With its burden of mystery
Cleaved to my passage.
Grace, like a grief assuaged,
A forgiven sin, beckoned
This dark angel to its shadow.
There is nothing the mind reckons
That the heart cannot undo:
See – the miraculous window
Of the water stands unbroken.

Miser

Over the bed's cliff my legs dangle.
It is always the day before dawn
At this hour, wishing myself an angel
Or a pebble – free fall, a way down

Without paying. Against gravity
The heart grapples – irons and hurled anchor
Scouring the air. Nothing will purchase poverty
So well as the clipped coin of hunger.

I shall go out on an empty belly,
Bequeathing to the future my past
And – lest I should sink without trace –
To my memory, love's ballast.

Anatomy of Departure

As the two ripe halves
Of a heart, our apportioned selves

Part cleanly at the thrill
Of the ball in the whistle's belly;

Only my child in the crook
Of your arm will not unhook

His gaze – exact, dispassionate –
From where I was, stepping out

Of my skin, my skeleton,
Bone by bone, dismantling.

Tyranny of Choice

Pick a card, any card
You'll say. I love this trick –
The tease and tyranny of choice –
The dove's tail tender
On your fine and hidden fingers,
And the thumb I'm under.

You know my Queen of Hearts
By the dog-ear on her top-left
Bottom-right corner;
By the voluptuous sad mouth
Which will not smile,
Whichever way you turn her.

Unguentarium

18. Unguentarium: bird. Italian
1st century A.D.

That night, all night, he lay on his back
Sleepless, watching the stars track
Like bubbles in the cool blue glass
That was his passion. By dawn
The bird had come to nest in the palm
Of his mind, almost weightless,
From the nib of its beak to the tail
A seamless sweep of apothecary blue.

And as the gaffers gossiped of the latest –
The loose woman washing with the unguent
Of her tears the strange man's feet –
He gathered into his lungs
All the faith of his marvellous new art,

And dipping the pontil into the molten glass
Blew life – the curve of the breast
Of the bird, swinging it through thin air
Down to the stone cold marver,
Burnishing; then again through fire

Retracing the tilt of the nape of her neck
As she stooped at her heart's business,
His lungs coaxing the pliant glass
And the bird-form blooming – into the vessel
That would bear the soul, the precise
Cast of the glass-blower's breath
Down two thousand years of incalculable loss
Intact, like some miraculous fossil.

Ribes rubrum

Light's rosary, blood-bright spheres:
They should be pendent from the ear
Of some cool woman of Vermeer.

The sun's glass worry-beads,
Jujube of July to the blackbird's
Elderberry eye – how they bleed

The hectic rose of its fever!
I thought I would stand there forever
With the green light washing over

Me, idle-handed, while the ribbed globe
Of each berry ripened its glow.
I suppose what held me was that slow

Transfusion of all the senses, leaving
Me shadowless, opaque, suspended of belief.
Until, that is, the blackbird lifted

In its epicurean bill
This sacrament, a single ruby
To the sun's dark crucible.

Contrary Motion

(FROM *Cosmos and Mimosa*)

Spreadeagled for sleep, godlike, on your back
In the long grass, after the close-hauled
Act, you lie willing the sky

To stand still. It's a confidence trick
You think (like faith, like sex, like all
Illusions of power) – when the key

Yields suddenly in the mind's lock
And the green raft slips its hausers,
Gliding back through the eye

Of unknowing. What lies in its wake,
In the ruffled skein of hours hauled
From the future, is a far cry.

Linda France

RUFUS FRANCE

Selection from: *Red* (1992), *The Gentleness of the Very Tall* (1994) and *Storyville* (1997).

LINDA FRANCE's three books chart highs and lows in lives and relationships, exploring the badlands of love and sex, tuning in to music and memory. Her poetry peels back layers of meaning in pursuit of honesty. 'There is much sensuous pleasure in the "skin" of things, and in language itself' (Carol Rumens). She is a poet seduced by extremes – equally at home with grit and velvet, greedy for rich imagery and exotic allusions. Many of her poems tread a tightrope between freedom and threat, violence and love, evoking a world under pressure – personal and political – and striving for balance and transformation with an uncompromising pragmatism. ●

Linda France writes:

I was born in Newcastle, and when I was five my family moved to Dorset. I trace my poetry back to that early dislocation, the keen awareness of language, of the power of words beyond what they actually say, a fascination with the sounds they make. I wrote 'North and South' after reading John Betjeman's verse autobiography *Summoned by Bells*.

I enjoy using fixed forms. I like their certainty, the sense of tradition, their music. 'Blues for Bird' is a variation on a sestina, with six-syllable lines to reinforce the "sixness" of the form. A maverick improvisation that seemed suitable for a poem about jazz saxophonist Charlie Parker.

When I become absorbed in working on a poem I feel it physically – a prickling sensation on my skin, a warm tightness in my belly, a sort of arousal – an intensified awareness that takes me somewhere else, raw and dynamic. It's always as if it were for the first time – risky, exciting, compelling and utterly necessary. 'Body Language' accentuates the eroticism of this process.

'My Muse, the Whore' and 'In Kind' are from a section called *On the Game* in *Storyville*. I was interested in exploring an institution that crudely played out the sexual dynamic of conditioning and trade-off, where "love" is a form of currency, only offered with some expectation of return; how we act out this lack of generosity and greed, based on fear, with other people and treat ourselves in the same harsh way. This was a painful series to write but I like poetry that guides the reader *and* the poet through unexplored territory.

North and South

Back in 1962 the world was
A foreign place I was just beginning
To feel at home in. I'd mouth and tongue sounds
My ears heard – Mam's clipped consonants, big sisters'
Sing-song vowels. And people understood.

Then one night was a dream of a red room
With wheels that kept me awake, stars spelling
South. South. South, where it never snowed and we
Would live in a nice new house and I would
Go to a nice new school.
                                        No one warned me.

Hamworthy Primary was full of kids
With straw between their teeth that made them sound
Like lazy cows. Where I came from the talk
Was quick as flocking birds. We laughed out loud –
No sneering behind hands, with rolling eyes.
Who's her? I cried inarticulate tears.

To survive, I had no choice but to try
To make my mouth echo back their fat *ain'ts*,
Become a chewing cow; or at least pretend.
I parroted their slow accents, even
Though the long feathers never really fit.
I plucked them out, the first chance I got;
But discovered I'd also lost, mid-flight,
My native accent I thought was bone.

In its place was this anonymous voice,
That sounds, to me, as if it belongs to
Someone else; feels two or three sizes too large.
The words and the spaces between the words
Ring with false echoes, false compass points.

Blues for Bird

What you did to the blues
was the sound of a bird
trapped behind broken glass
beating at the liquid
light, struggling to fly free.
You crushed bones with your horn.

They all told you a horn
shouldn't be blown that free
and fast. You played the blues
hot as neon, liquid
gas. Your sax and a glass
of booze – you were a bird.

And they called you *Yard bird*
too, singing back home blues
twitching that brassy horn
full of amber liquid –
those notes that shone like glass
made you dream you were free.

Say who of us is free?
We all live under glass
wishing we were bird,
sky gold with angel horn.
But we swim in the blues –
indigo, turquoise, liquid

as the sea. Your liquid
cocktail was spiked with horn
of horse. Nothing is free.
On the streets, doing bird
they followed you, those blues –
tears just mirrors of glass.

But still you'd fill your glass,
pick up, polish your horn.
The tune spilled like liquid
from your lips. You were free
as death – your soul a bird.
You earned your breath, your blues.

Bird, you're a ghost of glass,
liquid mid all those blues –
free at last, your horn, you.

Body Language

> '...*metaphors are dangerous. Metaphors are not to be*
> *trifled with. A single metaphor can give birth to love.*'
> MILAN KUNDERA

Before, she used to need a translator
to understand what his body language
signified, its present tense. She declined
the metaphor of eye contact, explored
the academic use of pseudonym.

Why is the alphabet in that order?
was one of many unsettling questions
provoked by the micofiche of letters,
dinner, too much whiskey. Bed was always
conditional; might be superlative.

When the VDU bleated *Insert, Text,*
Merge, she couldn't process the words on the tip
of her tongue, nipple, hip, solar plexus,
clitoris: the cowardice of one who
knew what systole meant, diastole, oscillation.

My Muse, the Whore

She is my right hand woman, my best friend. I know
I can only trust her as much as I trust myself.

She lounges around, pretending to be unavailable,
playing hide and seek, perfectly happy, smoking

better cigarettes than I can afford, fragrant, foreign,
filing her nails into french-polished almonds,

listening to women's voices on the radio, just
waiting for me to whistle. She's the best

lover I've ever had, the only one to deserve all
the attention she demands. Which I give freely,

our hands touching like the blue and yellow
of irises coupled in a tight-lipped vase, full

of sugar, or aspirin, to eke out their short time.
I pay her in American dollars, eagles. She never

complains; leaves me with the shape of a door,
a siphoned look about the eyes, skin crackling.

The way she strokes my palm makes me forget
the etiquette of dexterity, makes me surrender.

Our pulses are indigo streaks of lightning.
She whispers in my ear for more and more.

My left hand powders her cheek and thinks
of lilies, the taste of pollen on its five tongues.

I hear her laughing and it is an old sad song
I know the words to. She is an open book

with a marbled spine. I am the minder
of her scarlet heart. And I never tire

of listening to her stories, passing them on
like butterfly cakes in patterned paper cases.

We never use a microwave. Recharge the batteries
for our deluxe vibrator. What I like

about her is how she makes jokes
and doesn't care if nobody laughs. She isn't scared

to cry. We go back a long way, old friends
with a history that never dies. Always another trick.

In Kind

Such a gentleman, lowering black wool
on your shoulders, he bends to kiss the nest
of your neck, breathe in its dangerous scent.
Your white throat is wreathed with garlic jewels,
the empty cases of prawns. Then you know
you are to be his after-dinner mint,
his petit-four. Only your eyes say *no*
to what he's adding up. As if you count.

Pocketing his keys, he invites himself
in; needs the bite of black coffee before
skulking back to his wife, a mongrel home
from adventures. His braces stretch across
a three-course belly; five raw fingers
fork your crossed thigh. You know you want the prick
to leave; but he wants your share of the bill
he paid, insisting, *my dear*. His pleasure.

Your new settee's giving, getting smaller.
Acid vinaigrette curdles in your throat;
paella peppering your tongue. Heartburn:
a sour aftertaste. He unfolds your legs
like a napkin. Prefers it with the lights
on – the opposite of *no* – what he can't
have at home. You wake up alone, the bed
smelling of sweat, your own; the price of it.

Anne Rouse

ELIZABETH ROUSE

Selection from: *Sunset Grill* (1993), *Timing* (1997), and new work.

ANNE ROUSE is an American who has lived in London for the past 25 years, where she works as a freelance writer and mental health worker. She responds to contemporary urban culture both as a satirist and as a lyric poet. Many of her poems are hymns to the momentary and the marvellously futile, evoking adolescence and physical love, football and the office, misfits and conformists. Carol Rumens says 'a sardonic generosity permeates many of the poems about men'; Maura Dooley, that her poetry relies on 'wry insight and careful understatement: controlled, accurate, witty and effective language'. ●

Anne Rouse writes:

I tend to write about grey, unprepossessing places in North London. Much of 'Her Retirement' was composed in an underground station, when the words *Morden via Bank* on the destination signs began to sound like a refrain. Unlike clerks, secretaries are thinly represented in literature, it seems to me, and the repetitions of the villanelle quickly suggested the tipsy formality of a leaving party.

'England Nil' burst its way out of another, more conventional sonnet. Having discarded the first poem, except for the end-rhymes, I found myself writing about football violence. I've since been asked how a woman could meaningfully tackle such a laddish theme. The short answer is that there's probably a hooligan in me.

I enjoy satire, but I'm more drawn to the lyric. 'Virginian Arcady' followed a visit in a dream from a tall, glamorous, curiously attired woman. I took her for the embodiment of poetry, a warm but steely reminder to keep faith with the self. Recently I've been working on personal narratives and lyrics, with fewer external characters, but I'm also writing for theatre, and learning increasingly from other art forms.

Writing, for me, is an act of almost chemical precision, and the poem that results from a new mixture of words, intonations and pauses should be a little tumult, an event. Bob Cobbing, the contemporary sound artist, once remarked that the job of the poet is to defeat the machine. In order to override the scratchy gramophone of conventional thought, he or she must have explored a given poetic terrain as honestly and as sensitively as possible. The work itself should challenge, and connect.

England Nil

The advance to Hamburg broke with all the plans.
Doug spelled them out in Luton Friday night.
Someone had ballsed it up. A dozen vans
Waited in convoy, ringside. Blue and white
We stumbled through. The beer
When we found it in that piss-hole of jerries
Was all we needed. Who won the war,
Anyway? Who nuked Dresden? Two fairies
Skittered behind the bar, talking Kraut
Or maybe Arabic. We clocked the poison
Smiles and chanted till the SS threw us out.
Stuttgart was a tea-party to this. One
By one they've nicked us, berserk with fear.
You've been Englished but you won't forget it, never.

Spunk Talking

When men are belligerent or crude,
it's spunk talking, it's come come up for a verbal interlude:
in your face Jack, get shagged, get screwed, get your tits out,
get him, lads, bugger that, hands off, just you try it,
you're nicked, left hook, nice one Eric, hammer hard,
shaft him, stitch that, do you want to get laid or not, red card.
Spunk speaks in gutturals, with verbs. No parentheses.
Spunk's a young con crazy to break from Alcatraz.
Sonny, you'll go feet first. So spunk has to sing,
hoarsely, *The Song of the Volga Boatmen, I am an Anarchist,*
the Troggs' *Wild Thing.*
Cynthia Payne said, after her researches, not to be debunked,
that men are appreciably nicer when de-spunked.
Before time began the void revolved, as smooth and bored
as an egg, when a tiny ragged crack appeared,
and the world exploded like an umpire's shout,
as the primal spunk of the cosmos bellowed OUT!

Her Retirement

Just a little party, nothing swank,
I told the founder, but you know Mr B.
There are so many of you here to thank.

I leave you the later tube trains, dank
At the hand-rails from a human sea,
Dreaming down to Morden via Bank.

I've homed quietly to port while others sank,
By keeping at my stenography.
There are so many of you here to thank.

I scan the backs of houses, rank on rank:
The comfy lamps, the oblique misery
Streaming down to Morden via Bank.

Our gardens keep us from the abyss, I think.
With the cheque I'll buy a trellis, or a tree.
There are so many of you here to thank.

And unaccustomed as I am to drink,
I toast you all who follow me
– There are so many of you here to thank –
In dreaming down to Morden, via Bank.

The Uni-Gym

At a shout to a disco drum, the women dance
In sorbet cotton knits. Sweat darkening
On spines, they bend and reach.

In the stone chill of the gym downstairs,
Weightlifters howl, as if for sex,
Or pace, furtive in the room-sized mirror,

To meet gingerly in bed. His density
Helps him feel safer from the likes of her –
Whose heart is stronger now, and unforgiving.

Sacrificial Wolf

The careful suburban dead turn their backs
On this squat of sodden grass,
Hedged by the Finchley traffic:
The vicar poised like a prowhead
Over the shameless pit, answered
By a hectoring gull. It brings back
The afternoons in the dry houses,
The hostels and clinic waiting-rooms,
When you with the cor anglais of a shout
Parted the smokers' fug,
Flattering social workers with quotes
From Wilde or Krishnamurti –
Such was the splendour and disgrace,
That only a few of us have come to light
Our makeshift Roman candles, bitten shy:
An elegy, my friend, dear wolf,
Being just your sort of con.

Virginian Arcady

My muse came up from the creek,
Taller than a man in the speckled shade,
Where crayfish imitate tiny stones,
And the brisk water plays.

Reckon it was a muse, being so
Ringletty and fair, with a child's eye.
In her head-dress bitter, living grapes
Nest on the wild vine.

Strolling the bogged paths
Of the bottom field, apart by armslength,
She talked low, reproachful, pretty:
Said I don't love her enough.

Queynt

Hostage to the phalli,
where are your celebrations?
In the delivery suite;
among the porn queens?

Blood-warm and sea-brine,
maroon luxurious
rupture, your monuments
aren't theirs,

columns and Concorde; you've
only you, strong
as grass, sly mouth. Lewd
old thing.

Timing

Light hosanna'd in the mirrors.
We were double, multiple; but our quadrille
ended when you bowed and faded.

This evening in you walked – foot-sore, apologetic.
A minstrel, out of tune.
The sun had gone in, the room was brown

through the rattan blinds,
and I'm no coy languisher, no Penelope.
I'd done my scribbling in the book of you.

Sunday Morning

Blood sprouts like early spring
among the styrofoam burger cases and butt-ends
of the Seven Sisters Road.

It was Saturday night, swearing
and uplifted, who sent these vivid notes
to Sunday morning, its shrivelled twin;

a red path ending in the sturdy daylight,
when he rouses,
only to ache, and smile.

Lilies of the Field

You want corporate woman I get her for you
living doll on that billboard you like?
she got nice silicone, taped up brown eye shadow cleavage
skin by Max Factor and air brush
don't kid yourself even lights out she's a peach
spend how you like you may get her lay her
the modern world anything possible
telling your limerick on chat show
mama crying forgive her
and baby doll sucking her big eyes on you
da da   buy buy

Glass

You clambered into the glass of whisky
as the station bar was about to shut,
the tables curiously leaning into each other
like mates in a photo; the shutters scraped down,
a broom and dustpan flourished
with French hilarity, like the barman's goodbyes,
after a string of comforts, whiskey, Guinness,
heading off to pied-à-terre lodgings in Richmond;
no need for the unremarkable courage of the Dutch,
no glints in it; you are loved.

Moniza Alvi

MONIZA ALVI left Pakistan for England when a few months old. Her two OUP books, *The Country at My Shoulder* (1993) and *A Bowl of Warm Air* (1996), draw on real and imagined homelands in poems which are 'vivid, witty and imbued with unexpected and delicious glimpses of the surreal – this poet's third country' (Maura Dooley). In her later work, her delicately drawn fantasies transform the familiar into strange evocations of the joys and tensions of relationships, of love, intimacy, frustration, jealousy and paranoia, her rich imagery and luxuriant imagination recalling the transformations of Chagall paintings, the dream-visions of Douannier-Rousseau. ●

Selection from: *Carrying My Wife* (2000).

Moniza Alvi writes:

A new venture in my work has been a series of poems where I play the role of husband to an imaginary wife. In a sense the poems are autobiographical, and writing from a male or "husband" viewpoint has been a way of distancing myself from the sensations and difficulties portrayed, and then zooming in closely. I found surreal aspects of relationships emerged, and also the humour which might have been blurred in a head-on approach. In the end, I suppose, the poems do not show a male stance, but another way of looking at oneself. Current writing includes poems about the world of work, which are the beginning of a response to many years of school-teaching. So far I have concentrated on the stresses! Some of my most recent poems focus on the strange state of pregnancy and the responsibility of parenthood. I have continued the investigations into my Pakistani background which I began in my previous collections, this time touching on a kind of racial invisibility in the town where I grew up, and the "otherness" of growing up as a child of mixed origins.

When I first started writing seriously I was reading Angela Carter, Italo Calvino, and J.G. Ballard's science fiction. I am attracted by fantasy and the strange-seeming and find there some essence of experience. I feel an affinity with poets from a multi-cultural background, or those that have a multiracial identity such as Mimi Khalvati, Sujata Bhatt and Imtiaz Dharker. Other contemporary poets who have made a strong impression on me include Susan Wicks, Vicki Feaver and Selima Hill.

Missing

When my wife disappeared
it was grey as a school shirt.
When she vanished she switched names
backwards and forwards –
her own, her mother's, mine.
Hadn't she been orphaned, adopted,
rejected, married, divorced
and finally wedded to the stare
of the planets, the anxiety
of the constellations?
My wife was a rare occurrence
and a common occurrence.
She created a hiding place
in the empty supermarkets of the moon.
I called her a thousand times –
first with a map spread on my knees,
then with a tablecloth spread on my lap.
I remembered the phases of her dreams.
She had crossed the border.
Gone to a stormland, a scarlet landslide.
I expect she walks differently now,
rolls from side to side like a ship.
Clasps that child's bow and arrow
she took from the sideboard.

Fish

I envied my wife her nightly visions.
She'd lay each one proudly on the bed

like a plump, iridescent fish,
and ask me to identify it.

Some nights I'd even manage to trap
my own by concentrating hard,

submerging the net into blue-black waters.
I'd place my catch on the rippling sheet.

So we'd have our own two fish, almost
indecent, nuzzling each other's mouths,

soul-fish, awkward in our hands,
hungry, as if our lives were a host

of crumbs to gulp in greedily.
They'd beat their tails very fast

until we could only see the one dream
moving between us, or feel stirring

one enormous fish, with our own lives
grieving, joyful, growing in its belly.

Carrying My Wife

I carried my wife inside me –
like a cable car I pulled her
up the mountainside of our days.

I lifted her quite naturally
and I carried the floating,
prancing seahorse within her.

I took them both to the crossroads.
Stooping like St Christopher
I bore her – a slippery wave.

The hospital parted for us
strongly as the Red Sea.
I coaxed her through swings doors

which gusted to and fro
like our past and future.
She was sea-sick.

Sometimes she could hardly
remember who I was.
I only intended to leave her

for a moment in the bulrushes,
but she slept and slept,
hibernated like a star

gone to ground.
Then I carried her
to the ends of the Earth.

Backgrounds

Evenings, listening hard
I'd catch a sound I could barely identify.

Sometimes it would be soft as clouds meeting
or the sky seeming to touch the earth.

Then ear to the ground I'd realise
it was our backgrounds rubbing together

like warm hands, or dry sticks
which would eventually make a flame.

Countries which had once owned us
quivered with visions of my wife and me

wandering through them separately or together
aimless as cattle – I'd strain to hear

our pasts at war with each other,
county towns colliding, frayed at the edges.

There'd be the rumblings of our adventures.
I'd imagine my wife, struggling up to me,

laden with sacks of haldi,
or sacks of our vowels and consonants.

I'd view all the rooms we'd ever undressed in,
and watch us throw off our clothes – hardly

understood how we managed to let them go.
In cheerful moods I'd see all the garments

my wife had ever worn – they'd be dancing,
the jeans, pinafore dresses, salwar kameez.

I'd hear all the haircuts we'd ever had chiming.

Man Impregnated

And I envied her the baby within,
tried to cultivate my own –
first with a cushion to simulate the bump.
Then I gained weight, soon became
a man impregnated with light and dark,
with violet, with the wrong food,
with small bottles of beer.
I soothed and patted my own bump,
felt the delicious fullness of it,
the groaning weight of it – until
at last I awoke with a glass abdomen.

I peered into it constantly,
saw in miniature my wife and myself,
upside down, slotted neatly into each other.
I had no morning sickness,
shortage of breath or indigestion,
but pressing against my ribcage
were the feelings I could scarcely own,
the rough creatures which fed off me.
I'd ask my wife to place her pregnant ear
to my stomach and listen to the trauma of the sea,
throwing us up as driftwood on the beach.

Stephen Knight

STEPHEN KNIGHT's dark, unsettling poems look at things strangely, revealing surreal truths in external and internal worlds. His is a voice from 'the outskirts of Larkin country, grown shabbier, quirkier, more garish and desolate, but for all that, indestructible' (Joseph Brodsky). Poems both playful and touching in their exploration of mortality and faith in chaotic lives, they exhibit 'that kind of humour that is simply an alternative to a cry of pain. They are edgy, full of doubts, nostalgic but unsentimental' (Bernice Rubens). 'Their tone is very striking...urban, allusive, seriously jokey, formally dashing' (Andrew Motion). ●

Selection from: *Flowering Limbs* (1993) and *Dream City Cinema* (1996).

Stephen Knight writes:

I was born in Swansea and began to write around the time my family moved closer to the sea. My earliest poems sprouted from a long-haired adolescence of morose, clifftop walks; and water seeps into my writing to this day.

My taste for quotidian surrealism owes as much to a boyhood love of Marvel and DC comics as it does to my later enjoyment of writers – Swift, Kafka, etc – whose perspectives are, in all senses, funny. Mermaids, monstrous faces in the curtains that hung in my bedroom when I was small, or a 1980s news report about the trade in human organs are among the germs of poems in the following selection.

Displacement, surfaces and a weak purchase on solid ground also figure, which may have something to do with being the Welsh son of an Austrian mother, the source of a not unpleasant sense of separateness throughout my childhood. While I can suggest origins, however, outcomes are (for me) necessarily vague. I wouldn't bother to travel if I knew the destination beforehand, and the day I fully understand my reasons for writing is the day I stop.

The Eyeball Works

Ad-men bandy slogans, like *PUPILS GUARANTEED...*
The would-be donors queue all afternoon
while tinted windows of The Eyeball Works run cloud
and passer-by at half their normal speed.
Into the evening, noises draw a crowd −
footsteps on a flight of marble stairs;
murmurs from an unlit foyer and the slow,
self-satisfied give of drapery and armchairs
laundered to the colour of the moon.
Noses flatten on the glass like dough.

Inside, the Eyeball Brochures packed in crates
whiff, unmistakably, of Money and Success;
they leave from the dock doors every night
with details of bargains and sell-by dates.
The workers, clothed in dust-revealing white,
wear gloves that cling and oblong paper hats,
each stamped with a Happy Eyebrows trademark.
For safety's sake, they stand on rubber mats −
before their lightly-greased machines − to press,
drill, gouge and slice until it's dark.

The marble benches are cobbled with eyes
arranged in rows then opened like books;
eyes jostle in dishes, eyes bob in jars
labelled according to status and size.
Eyes for Librarians and *Eyes of the Stars*
anticipate one of those numerous tinges
(from Palimpsest Azure to Paul Newman Blue)
stored in carboys, doled out through syringes.
Every jar is packed with long, blank looks
and the needles are true.

Tonight, Security is a humming sound
and the smell of disinfectant damp on floors.
Tonight, the door knobs are electrified
and the ugly dog let loose in the compound
pads down corridors like a bride...

Small cameras on the ceilings wink and weave
while, tapping the walls with his complimentary stick,
the last of the donors to leave
is 'leaving' through the NO ADMITTANCE doors.
He waves Goodbye. The doors go tick, tick, tick.

Double Writing

Sea View, Water's Edge, Atlantis,
lugubrious Guest Houses welcome the tide

after dark, from the opposite side of the road.
Their windows are lit with VACANCIES.

At closing time, Covelli's chips do a roaring trade
though his name has flaked from the side of the building.

Tighter than fists in the gaps in wooden benches,
pages of the local paper soak in vinegar.

Wind sizzles through trees
while, from the promenade, waves reach for the last bus

back into town. Ticking over in the back seat,
somebody sleeps it off. His thumb is in his mouth.

The timetable never works
and graffiti spreads through the shelter like wires –

refinements of a thick, black autograph
above the spray of glass, below the one-armed clock.

In West Cross garages, drums, guitars and microphones
huddle together, waiting to be famous.

Things go quiet. Things are unplugged.
Cutlery is laid out for the morning.

In Case of Monsters

On the way to bed **a)** Take the staircase
slowly. Note how many steps. Never race
to the landing or try to chase
shadows into corners.

b) Place books and comics under your bed –
The Bible is still a safe bet. **c)** Spread
Sheffield knives two feet from your head.
Polish them first. Ask Dad

nicely and he may sharpen them for you.
d) Always *jump* into bed: monsters queue
behind the valance until dew
curdles on the garden.

e) Face the door before you go to sleep.
Remain like that all night. Use string to keep
yourself in place then **f)** Count sheep
to save strain on the knots.

NB Always have your bed well away
from windows and let the room breathe all day
but never, never when the grey
evenings give way to night.

g) Watch the pattern in your curtains change
to things at sunset altogether strange.
In the silence, they rearrange
their disenfranchised smiles.

When you hear your heartbeat on the pillow
h) Count every thump, and if you don't know
now the number of steps to go
before your blood arrives

i) Check the knives.

The Big Parade

Here they come past High Street station, everyone I've ever known
and some I've only seen on television, marching three abreast,

my Junior School Headmistress at the front – Miss Morgan
with her bosoms now as much a shelf as when I saw her last

it must be thirty years ago – hurling to the sky a silver baton
(twirling up it tumbles earthwards like the prehistoric bone

in Kubrick's *2001*): turning at the Dizzy Angel Tattoo Studio
down Alexandra Road then into Orchard Street they go,

my other teachers – Grunter, Crow and Mister Piss on stilts –
juggle furry pencil-cases, worn board-dusters, power balls,

there's Adam West, his Batman outfit taut around his waist,
and then the Monkees, Mickey hammering a drum the others

blowing on kazoos: they navigate the Kingsway roundabout
to pass the Odeon where everyone is dropping ticker-tape

a storm of paper falls on Malcolm in a stripy tank-top, John
and Hugh and catches in the hairnet of our loony neighbour

Nestor – keeping up despite an ancient Zimmer frame –
and Bill the communist and Mister Shaddick, hirer of skips,

his brown bell-bottoms crack and snap around his platform shoes,
the collar of his paisley-patterned shirt's two giant set-squares

look! a girl from Pennsylvania who kissed me once, still thirteen
after twenty years, I shouldn't recognise her smile and yet I do,

I call to her but she's too far away, atop a jewelled elephant
she's waving to the crowd like someone fresh from outer space:

travelling along St Helen's Road towards the sea, the cheers,
the noises of the instruments resounding through the city centre

out, past vinyl three-piece suites and lava lamps in Eddershaws
go Mary Dorsett, Julie Dolphin, Tony (very much alive),

Rhiannon then a row of faces I can't put a name to now
but still I wave and shout and watch them disappear,

the boy who butted me one break-time skulking at the back,
the music fading, blurring with the gulls, the sea, the sounds

of people going home, till everywhere I look
the streets are quiet as a fall of snow.

The Surf Motel

Across the waves that vague, moss-covered knell
Drifting from The Surf Motel
's the dinner bell.

Starfish pack the car park at the height of every swell.

As always, every peal
Calls forth another conger eel
To nibble at the edges of the evening meal.

Silt and seaweed feast upon the carpets they conceal.

All evening, cleaners bail
Black water out of poky rooms to no avail –
Their patience and their buckets fail.

In hoover bags, like escapologists, fish flail

But still,
While tides will ruin everyone they fill,
Visitors remain for weeks, for years perhaps, until; until.

The cost of staying blurs on every bill.

The Mermaid Tank

Beneath my weight, the duckboards bow.
   Two buckets, slopping water, weigh me down.
A cold wind howls around the cages now,
   While rain sweeps in – across the town –
Again; and while our rheumy-eyed,
    Arthritic monsters fall asleep
       Or vegetate
         I kneel beside
The Songstress Of The Deep
    And wait.

All afternoon, the punters pass
   Her tank in single file; because it's dark
Inside, they press their faces to the glass.
   I breathe, at night, on every mark.
Behind my cloth, the water churns
    And curls around our fat dugong
      And when it clears
        (Like smoke) she turns
Away, and any song
   I hear

Is 'just the wind' or 'my mistake'...
   Outside, discarded handbills catch their wings
On tents or in the mud while, in their wake,
   Paper cups, ticket stubs and things
The rain dismantles every night
    Turn cartwheels in the foreign air
      Before they throng
        The sky, too light
To settle anywhere
   For long.

Katie Donovan

PETER SELLERS

Selection from: *Watermelon Man* (1993) and *Entering the Mare* (1997).

KATIE DONOVAN belongs to a cosmopolitan generation of younger Irish poets: much travelled, with broad cultural references and with American poets as her formal models, but drawing on Irish mythology and stories of her own family forebears. Her 'taut, challenging, deliberate poems' (Eileen Battersby) trace the female principle, exploring the hungers which haunt both our flesh and our fantasies: the conjunction of myth and the physical world of body and earth. 'Katie Donovan has staked out a territory, the womanly erotic' (Carol Rumens), homing in on 'the wildness of the instant of emotion' (Éilean Ní Chuilleanáin). ●

Katie Donovan writes:

Although I do write poems about love and the body, I find the description 'womanly erotic' limiting and one-sided. My work deals with myth, history, religion, desire, superstition, hunger, as well as with my travels. I am interested in pre-Christian Ireland, when mythic Goddess figures were autonomous, powerful, libidinous and very physical. In short, much better role models than anything our repressive brand of Christianity has offered Irish women.

'Underneath Our Skirts' illustrates in a sardonic fashion what I mean by repressive Christianity. It was inspired by a friend's wedding, during which I discovered that my period had started. I grew indignant as I thought of how a woman's menstrual blood – the fertile blood of life – is deemed unclean in the Christian tradition, whereas Christ's blood, the barren blood of a dying man, is worshipped and fetished. 'Entering the Mare' shows show pre-Christian Ireland continued on its merry way right into the twelfth century, with the nominated chieftain being forced to enter and consume the embodiment of the Goddess, the white mare, before he could assume power. An early and brutal form of Communion. The Earth Goddess was worshipped in the form of a horse in both Ireland and Wales (where she was known as Epona).

My day job as a journalist often gives me ideas for poems, from interviewing gamblers to researching the destruction of the ozone layer. Visual art, colour and landscape have a strong appeal. The many facets of my relationships are a constant inspiration, as the two other poems included here will illustrate.

Underneath Our Skirts

Although a temple
to honour one man's voluntary death,
his ceaseless weep of blood,
the women cannot enter
if they bleed —
an old law.

As the bridal couple glides
down the aisle,
her white veil twitching,
I feel my pains.
A woman
bleeding in church,
I pray for time,
for slow motion.
Unprotected, I bleed,
I have no bandage,
my ache finds no relief.
My thorns
are high heels
and itchy stockings.
He, the imitator, bleeds on
in numb eternal effigy,
his lugubrious journey of martyrdom
rewarded with worship.

Tonight custom demands more blood:
sheets must be stained
with the crimson flowers
of a bride's ruptured garden.
Her martyrdom
will be silent knowledge
suffered in solitude.

As we leave the house
of the male bleeder,
I feel myself wet and seeping,
a shameful besmircher of this ceremony
of white linen
and creamy-petalled roses;

yet underneath our skirts
we are all bleeding,
silent and in pain,
we, the original
shedders of ourselves,
leak the guilt of knowledge
of the surfeit
of our embarrassing fertility
and power.

These Last Days

I cartwheel like a knife
into the sagging canvas of now –
it's a strange underwater dance,
all weed and drift –
my arrow nose shafts through
hunting you.

Like a whirlwind
coning down,
I'm peeling the brittle skin
of these last days
without you;

only in your arms
will I slowly open
the moist, seeded centre.

Entering the Mare

She stamps and shivers,
her white coat vainly shrugging,
as the would-be chieftain
plunges in, burying deep
his puny, acrid man's seed,
between her fragrant haunches.

The Goddess lives
in her fine rearing head,
the pink stretch of her lips,
the wide, white-haired nostrils.
Her hoof
might have crippled him,
her tail
whipped out his arrogant eyes.
Instead she jerks clumsily,
trying to escape
the smell of his hand.

Later he swims
in the soup of her flesh,
sucking on her bones,
chewing the delicate morsels
of her hewn body.

He has entered the Goddess,
slain and swallowed her,
and now bathes in her waters –
a greedy, hairy, foetus.

Rising from her remains
in a surge of steam –
her stolen momentum –
he feels a singing
gallop through his veins:
a whinnying, mane-flung grace
rippling down his spine.

Riding off on the wings
of the divine Epona,
he lets loose his dogs
to growl over her skeletal remnants,
the bloody pickings
in the bottom of his ceremonial bath.

*The inauguration of an Irish chieftain, as observed by
Geraldus Cambrensis (Gerald of Wales) in the 12th century.*

Grooming
(for my mother)

Dreamy and docile you sit,
as I comb out
the long ends of your hair.
Like mine, it is thin and straight –
a hairdresser's nightmare.

I have played with your hair
since I was scarcely
tall enough
to reach your reclining shoulder.
My small hands,
busy with their child's work,
seemed to comfort you.

Now you sit, slackly,
sighing as I pat and snip;
the brown swatches fall,
veined with grey: a splash
of last year's growing months.
Your face is delicate and girlish
as I guide the angles of your head.
My palms push you into reverie,
my pulls and swipes,
my amateur measurings,
my fussy trim.

It is a clumsy job.
Yet, as always, you shake yourself,
toss out the flattened strands,
and pronounce yourself glad.

Regretfully, you rise,
and go to sweep
the chopped grey-brown fluff
of your shorn locks,
as though cleaning out
the cluttered bedding
of a staled nest.

Chris Greenhalgh

Selection from: *Stealing the Mona Lisa* (1994) and *Of Love, Death and the Sea-Squirt* (1999).

CHRIS GREENHALGH's poems sparkle with irreverent comedy, exploring modern media society and personal experience, playfully conflating accurate satire and sensuality, eroticism and tenderness. Yet often beneath the glittering surface there is a sour, unsettling subtext as well as intimations of a darker tone. '*Lively* isn't an active enough word to encompass the man's range of moods, style, and specific bees-in-bonnet; *ebullient* comes closer. Sheer brilliance of language carries its own zest in easy intimacy. Greenhalgh writes with all his senses alert...Satiric wit and earthy humour come easily to him' (Bill Turner). ●

Chris Greenhalgh writes:

In many ways, I hope the poems speak for themselves and generate their own associative life. If they do possess a stylistic agenda, however, then I suppose it is this: to synthesise vivid imagery with the kind of narrative excitement more commonly experienced in fiction. Poetry has settled too readily for the trajectory of the elegy and the dying fall – that note of expiration which is the plangent echo of poetry's own decline in literary significance. For me, the lyric is just as much about mobilising the strategies of fiction.

I want my poems to have characters, a feeling for narrative rhythm and pace, together with a linguistic surface which, in its rapid changes of register and mood, reflects the discontinuities of modern life.

The poems garnered here, and in my published books, seek to move and amuse, to exhilarate and to provoke. At once passionate and ironic ('My Funny Valentine'), there is something here to offend everyone, and something, I hope, to delight everyone, too. Their common territory lies somewhere in that hinterland between private and public space, the space inhabited uneasily by Monroe ('The Night I Met Marilyn'), cruelly exposed by a photograph ('The Big No-No') and a suicide's video ('Of Love, Death and the Sea-Squirt'). Peppered with sensuality and satire ('A Man in the Valley of Women') and shot through with dark comedy, the poems may be playful, but I also wish them earnestly to be tender and true.

The Big No-No

The erotic tension is almost palpable
as they stand jiggling brandy loin-high

in warm circles: the corpulent older man
with the bonhomie of a department-store Santa,

his right arm draped round a young man's shoulders,
his left arm circling a younger woman's waist.

His glasses, at an oblique angle to the camera,
have whited-out, while the pupils of the other two

are pink as rabbits' eyes from the flash –
and if I tell you that the older man

happens to be my boss, the girl his mistress,
the other me, and that several times

her labia have given me less trouble
than a milk-carton, then perhaps you will

understand why I'm no longer employed
and why I finger this photograph with

three parts nostalgia, one part regret.

The Night I Met Marilyn

> 'Ask not what your country can do for you, ask
> what you can do for your country.'
> JOHN F. KENNEDY

The night I met Marilyn it was raining,
for I remember her petulantly shaking
her hair free from a scarf,
                and that pampered animality

in response to the cold – part come-on, part disdain,
the dangerously volcanic glamour of a mouth that
lured you to the lip, and caused you to fall in.

She had us all mesmerised, resembling a stack
of televisions in an electrical store,
all receiving the same programme;
yet behind the lazy sensuality and insouciance,
the gloved white finger quizzical against the chin,
it was obvious – to me anyway – there lay
a quiet centre of hurt, an abject vulnerability.
As she looked at me, I recognised
the management behind her smile,
and she seemed to understand that I understood.

I registered in her a terrible need for love,
and what happened later that evening
I have never related.
It would have been like stealing the Mona Lisa.

I promised Marilyn that in her all-too-public life,
the privacies that we, at least, shared
would be respected.

Then that last calamitous August night:
coming home, I heard the phone
insistent behind the locked door.
By the time I had found my key
and made a grab for the receiver,
                                    the phone was dead.

As at the ripple-ends of an earthquake,
the shock came sometime after the event,
yet it remains a painful, intractable thought even now,
and one which I have kept secret for over thirty years.

I will say no more, other than that the oblique details
and veiled portrait of the woman I knew and understood –
feisty, ardent, marketable –
can be found in the eponymous heroine
of my latest novel, *Marilyn Runmoe*, published tomorrow:
hardback £16.99, paperback £7.99 with 20 b/w photos.

A Man in the Valley of Women

He was captured in the Valley of Women.
They manacled his ankles and chained his wrists.
His captors pinioned him. One held his head.
Another picked up a needle and thread.

'What are you going to do?' he asked.
She played the needle over a candle flame.
'Sew both your lips together!' she laughed,
trailing a finger between his shoulder-blades.

She teased the needle through his upper-lip,
and drew his flesh together with silk-twine.
He felt the pressure of her fingertips
as her nails dug deep into his spine.

Slowly they broke all the bones in his feet.
The blood was used to rouge his cheeks.
His testes made an executive toy,
his glans a novelty cork for the wine.

Seized by the throes of change, he was aware
of a contending self, radically other;
an abrupt warping, a cruel deflection
of his sex from masculine to feminine.

The next few months, they fed him on jasmine
which stirred the female wings inside his breasts.
His ankles grew slimmer. His hair shone.
His vagina fermented like yeast.

A musk clung to his body. Unmistakable.
His clitoris thickened like a tonsil.
Buttermilk and aloe dissolved his Adam's apple.
His voice modulated to a falsetto.

They plucked every dark hair from his face
and pencilled his eyebrows until they were perfect.
They painted his lips in arresting shades,
and squeezed him into a whalebone corset.

Finally, he was ready for the Queen's birthday.
His hips swivelled pertly, his backside swayed.
'Tsk tsk!' went the other courtiers slyly.
'That's a frisky one,' he heard them say.

He burst from the cake, high-kicking through the icing,
swanking bridally from the marzipan.
Later, the Queen bid him kiss her ring.
She sighed: 'To think that once you were a man...'

My Funny Valentine

Those first days, making love above your father's study,
he would cough
so often in synchrony with your bliss
as to suggest a certain psychic discomfort.

I still remember that Valentine's, he took us out to dinner:
some high-priced, low-ceilinged Italian place.
As a waiter waggled a huge pepper-mill over
our plates, abruptly the pressure of the unspoken

broke. The word 'marriage' was broached
with the deft solemnity of a man handling high-grade uranium.
After several glasses of wine, we all began to glow.
A blue vein pulsed at his temple as he spoke.

Hypnotised by the wax dripping from the candle
and congealing between my fingers,
I conjured *a garlicky moon, a suitcase,*
you squeezing through the windowframe,

the lemonstain headlamps of the Citroën
strafing the walls of your parents' bedroom
*before tilting into the night...*Outside,
snow pecked at the window. The shadows

of leaves made flat dark hearts against the wall.
The web of wax between my fingers cracked.
The candle flames staggered in a sudden draught,
your eyes picking up flecks of yellow as gold.

My legs twitched like a pinioned insect's.
And sure enough, by the spring,
the light struck rainbows off your diamond ring.
By the summer we were married and, by the fall,

your operatic cries of joy
might have been heard by the neighbours
but for the double-glazed caulked storm-windows
prudently installed against the winter cold.

Of Love, Death and the Sea-Squirt

Hoping publicly to humiliate her husband,
she filmed herself swallowing whiskey and pills.

That night, watching in snowy low-grade colour
his wife's self-slaughter reproduced,

he fast-forwarded through all the abuse,
but stopped when she spoke of the sea-squirt,

listening with a sympathetic taste of acid on his tongue
to details of the creature's lifelong

search for a rock to make its home;
then the hideous consummation

as it set about eating its own brain.
That was the only part he watched again.

Ann Sansom

Selection from: *Romance* (1994) and new work.

ANN SANSOM's poetry overturns the reader's expectations, as in her choice of book title, *Romance*, and the title-poem itself, showing how we believe what we want to believe. Her poems often present human dramas in which people are seen as acting out their versions of themselves in their own fictions – what Stanley Cook called 'an authentic Northern mix of realism and imagination'.

'Sansom's poems often turn round and bite themselves, or their readers...their predominant register is one of brisk authenticity spiked with brash tabloid demotic...brisk authenticity and affectionate generosity' (Neil Powell). ●

Ann Sansom writes:

Any good ideas I have are for plays or, more likely, for the pleasure of thinking about. Poems tend to arrive with a phrase or a word I can't quite shake off. Sometimes a couple of lines, but rarely more than that. It's the process of writing that generates or releases the rest. The beginnings are always disorderly and not much survives the first draft. Trains, late hours and having a rowdy house are helpful. I've become adept at stealing time to read, write and idle.

'Voice' came from a song I was concocting on my way home one night. I knew there'd be a message waiting from a friend who'd fallen in love and stopped being witty. I was revving myself up to sympathy, getting all the venom out with the sibilants. It coincided with a new ansaphone and five kittens who liked to cosy on the red light, and record themselves snoring. Incoming voices made them pee in terror, breaking the messages: *don't forget the 19th* hiss *I'm sorry to bother you again but* hiss *by no means stay at Killadoon Hotel* hiss. It's been good to me since, this poem, once appearing on the back of the Russian *Vogue* – to advertise a red shirt (search me).

'Romance' started from *that night at Gallagher's*. I'd remembered it as the flashpoint for an appalling unnecessary argument. It was only in writing that I understood why she'd offer her own version regardless of his. At seven or eight you want grown-ups to keep the peace; older, you're entitled to laugh out loud.

All these poems, I think, were a coming to terms, a means of investigating an obsession with courtesy, obedience, defiance: aiming to grow up. I blame the Jesuits. Or would if I had time.

Romance

This is how he made her fall
in love with him. This is the tale
he always tells when he feels like talking.
The long one with the happy ending.

How he came by his sons, his daughters
our bold fathers, our pretty mothers
and the increasing shifting numbers of us.
This is where he finally won the prize

he wanted more than anything. She comes in,
her arms full, heading for the kitchen.
Awhile here, girl. I'm after telling them about
the night at Gallagher's I played the flute.

Now, surely to God, you remember that?
He winks to us, in no doubt. *I remember it –*
not breaking her long stride, smiling – *Indeed I do.*
And a terrible thing it was, if I may say so now.

He waits till she's gone. Remember this.
You never touch a Mayo tinker's bitch.
Nor any kind of laughing brazen
red-haired hard-of-hearing woman.

Confinement

That winter the stairs were always unlit.
Home late from work, I'd feel my way,
unlock the door by touch
and before I pressed the switch look up, wait
to see my lamp put out a saucer to the dark.

The skylight was almost clear then,
night came down to it at once,
a movement quick and weighty as water.

At first I'd count you by the moon, by my own fingers,
half believing I could feel you in my skin.
Then it snowed for weeks, accumulating on the glass,
filtering a tracing paper air. A diffuse frost
charged the constant underwater I crossed and crossed
mindless as a swimmer, keeping time for you.

At night, in the cold sheets, unable to sleep
I began to count you in days and hours,
I named you, held your head, your feet,
felt you turn in my own body heat.

Tonight, you've slept for twenty years.
I leave an overheated house, go out
into the cold backyard for air.
A neighbour calls me to the fence to watch.
He's opening the ice on his pond. The fish come up
preserved by their cold blood, their trust.

I close a frozen room on you, your placid drowning face.
and listen to my neighbour, who has learned to wait,
obedient to the rules that govern living things.
We share a cigarette and then discuss
the nature of confinement and release.

Voice

Call, by all means, but just once
don't use the *broken heart again* voice;
the *I'm sick to death of life and women
and romance* voice *but with a little help
I"ll try to struggle on* voice

Spare me the promise and the curse
voice, the ansafoney *Call me, please
when you get in* voice, the *nobody knows
the trouble I've seen* voice; the *I'd value
your advice* voice.

I want the how it was voice;
the *call me irresponsible but aren't I nice* voice;
the *such a bastard but I warn them in advance* voice.
The *We all have weaknesses
and mine is being wicked* voice

the *life's short and wasting time's
the only vice* voice, the *stay in touch,
but out of reach* voice. I want to hear
the *things it's better not to broach* voice
the *things it's wiser not to voice* voice.

Prince
(for Andrew Stibbs)

I study the board like the rules of a dead language
to be memorised, tried on the edge of the tongue
but not applied, not usefully, not this time of night
with the last train shunted out and the porters absent,
cosy, brewing up behind their mirrored door.

Snowed in once, they offered me a drop of whisky
in a mug of orange tea. Not tonight
because rain's a different element;
no camaraderies for those who're wet and late,
victims of their own persistent gullibility.

That time, at least I had a book, Machiavelli.
I read it twice. The station stray snored at my feet.
I got organised and ruthless overnight,
learned how human affairs are governed;
above all else, be wary of benevolent advice.

Tonight it's the *Rotherham Star* or nothing,
fragile and damp from the bin. Letters, small ads,
garden fork, one tine missing, excellent condition;
Massage and Sauna for Business Gents,
Adult Videos, a double spread of Lonely Hearts.

The realpolitik: *fortune is changeable*
like a woman – or an April timetable –
but a man of goodwill is obstinate
and usefully predictable, a snooty dog
that comes to heel. Good boy. At least I know your name.

The world is everything

Where I come from the language is water,
the essential beat of a line is tidal,
a sweep of blood to the heart
before the slow boom of a mother's voice
and her outer voice that breaks
to let others in, for manners.
The rhythm is sleep and turn in sleep
and rock awake and rest.
There is tedium without idleness.

Where I come from the ocean is pink
and framed and warm; belly breast face
an unclaimed inheritance as we roll
and flex in that roundness, lithe and slick,
trouble undreamed before us,
our only distress a thumb lost to the lips
a surge of spite in a tangled cord.

Where I come from we love our dark life;
we won't give it up, though we all leave.
There's no question of betrayal.
We develop a selective personal amnesia,
and deny the maps and diagrams we half believe
as if we might in fantasy have been there,
nothing more. Our hearts steady, our eyes clear
and our tongues begin to dry and falter.

Tracy Ryan

WENDY J KINSELLA

Selection from: *The Willing Eye* (1999).

TRACY RYAN is one of Australia's finest younger poets. Her third collection, *The Willing Eye*, is her first to be published in Britain. A freelance writer, she lives in Cambridge.

Dorothy Hewett has written that 'in Tracy Ryan's poems there are no safe houses, the walls of domesticity keep falling in and she is the clear-eyed tightrope walker negotiating a perilous foothold'. She often takes a small event and captures its nature as a borderline, sacramental experience. Hers is a flayed poetry, open to the shocks and pleasures of seeing and daily life, driven by a fascination with the shifting and precarious boundaries between the self and the world. ●

Tracy Ryan writes:

The personal and the external worlds interest me equally: the division between them seems false to me like, sometimes, the division between persons. I am interested in bodies, in overcoming the tendency to write as if words were disembodied and immaterial.

'Enough' arose from talking with a friend who has spent her life in nursing and who has often furnished me with practical information that sparks poems. But it arises more fundamentally, like many of my poems, from the idea of death. It's meant as a twist on the love song, locating love in the ability to survive. Living seems to me a process of loss, whether for good or bad. 'Spin' is thus about risk, about casting one's lot with another person, joyride rather than journey, a motorbike made to take three rather than one.

The two eclipse poems came from a collaboration with my husband, who also lived through these events as a child. The solar eclipse of 1974 was a huge marker in our imaginations, much like the moon-landing for a more global audience. The 'we' of these poems, though, is my own first family, including a brother mad on astronomy who lived only to the brink of adulthood. All this belongs to a world shut away with him, the stars a spiritual zone beyond reach. Both poems invoke Plath as the unavoidable moon-poet, and less directly owe something to Emily Brontë. They are about vision too.

The last poem, 'Trompe l'œil', is about the fallibility of vision, about how we make art regardless, and about death again! Yet I don't *see* myself as a gloomy poet...

Enough

You sleep on one side, your spine
the spine of a closed book,
your immaculate symmetry
folded in on itself,
the inside mysterious as
a Rorschach blot.
But the nurse laughs at aesthetics,
says our doubling
is designed for survival, the world
being full of people who walk about
with one lung, for instance,
labouring under the weight
of absence yet looking no different
from the rest of us. And yes,
if death or something more necessary should
sever us, I'd continue just
like that – taking in, I imagine,
only half the air but still enough.

Spin

Holding us all at once, I watch
this green world over your shoulder while
my daughter, wedged between us, can only
see sideways, the price of flying
over these soft contour banks that look
safe but would nonetheless crack
any bones we offered.
Unhelmeted, we ride
the borders of oatfields
yielding to wind like the tread of some
spectre I cannot follow,
my feet thrust in the bike's flanks
as if in stirrups
for a difficult birth. I believe

these roads know you just as
my body at night knows your body
will never hurt me. Your faith
inspires: breathes in & restores, even as
that wind tries
to distort our words.

Eclipse, Kenwick, 1974

It descended one schoolday
when we were children,
this darkness, the one condition
that enabled seeing
the element we turned in
yet allowed only partial vision:
bright ring, emblem of burning
bush and stark completion
slow-motion moon imposing
'O-gape of complete despair'
which is there, which is always
there; how we cherished
our little images,
pin-hole and television –
ersatz knowledges –
unaware you'd swallow year after
year after year and the one of us
who said, 'I am not afraid
to die because then I will see
the stars as I've always wanted.'
I have never forgotten
how still it was,
how the animals took on oddly
the same way they did
one summer, the day he died;
uneasy calm before that dry
and silent storm.
How we ate, drank and were merry
instead of lessons, and the teachers
told stories and pulled down the blinds.

Lunar Eclipse

'I shall be useful when I lie down finally'
— SYLVIA PLATH

When we were young we'd lie outside at night
because the heat drove us from beds sweat-soaked
as if life were leached & condensed from us
while we tried to sleep, even sheets too dense
for the body's escape. Flat on our backs
in buffalo grass & sand we imagined
the truth: we lay upright on a planet
facing other planets hung in the vast
blackness – not horizontal under sky
but part of it. All footholds slippery,
grounding provisional, the earth was then
a vehicle over whose actual course
we'd no control, we had to travel blind.
One night we felt ourselves obliterate
even the mirrored light the moon allowed,
our backs turned on the sun in what was like
an endless moment, but would soon be gone.
Now that I'm older I no longer sleep
outdoors, but know whenever I lie down
the walking world's a travesty & what
seems big in it is barely there at all.

Trompe l'œil

Look how the table's becoming
a table again,
as coach turns to pumpkin
only slower.

The marquetry's starting
to separate, making
rips in the fabric
of deception

just as my face takes rifts
under the same old daily
make-up, flesh begging
to differ.

It's as if the picture
were failing
through lack of someone's
faith

but who is it asking?
Who was that letter meant for
& what were the downturned cards
about to tell?

Our fingers want
to pick them up
but slip on glaze
rebarbative as mirrors,

itch over coins, quill, signet
& sealing wax.

Some kind of hoax.
Was it a joke only contemporaries
were meant to get,

an innocent talking point,
favourite set-piece?
Or did Boilly suspect we'd stand here
two centuries later
by his elaborate *memento mori*
still marvelling at his virtual skill,

the willing eye
a hopeless romantic that
can only be cheated?

Maggie Hannan

MOIRA CONWAY

Selection from: *Liar, Jones* (1995).

MAGGIE HANNAN writes quirky, offbeat poems which invite readers to share her delight in using language almost as an artist's material – which will yield clues to meaning or identity the more she works with it, subjecting the medium itself to playful interrogation. 'Her poetry grips language itself, making it both subject and object of many of her poems. She is inventive, playful and knowing: the poems glitter with an intelligent dark humour' (Maura Dooley). 'The situations of her poems reveal an obsessive interest in how, when, where and why meaning occurs between individuals, between individuals and the world' (David Kennedy). ●

Maggie Hannan writes:

Much of the work in *Liar, Jones* explores the idea that we are all, in some fundamental way, created by language. The two poems here imagine the voices of people who might ordinarily be silent in the face of the discourses which define them.

The first is about the experience of life modelling, a job which I did for many years. Sometimes students ask the model to pose in ways which evoke particular paintings or styles. In the poem, the model describes this process through the work of artists Schiele, Matisse and Freud. In the final part, she imagines using the work of American feminist photographer Cindy Sherman, who always uses herself as a model. The poem moves through the static and predetermined positions of the earlier painters to the more fluent and violent imagery of Sherman, whose work examines femininity and the manner in which women are represented.

The second is about an elderly psychiatric patient in one of the old hospitals, who was reluctant to communicate except through his own idiosyncratic sign language and a single, endlessly repeated phrase. He was an extraordinary man: ironic, witty, and ultimately joyful.

Both pieces are sequences and in this way try to capture the restlessness and unreliability of the different narratives. I try to give the subject–matter space to inhabit the different perspectives while compressing the language to the point where the unexpected is allowed to happen...a surprise association, a misleading echo, a reassessment of meaning. I want the poems to sound unsettling; I want them to hang like mobiles on the page.

Life Model

1 *Like Schiele*

Look − up and tangle
the flexion of shanks,

the dapple my hand
rakes, my hair, the air

the light is passing
through to blood

that cools and plots
its course.

This skin's
a thermogram they read

from: ochre, jade
and puce. To pull,

to hook myself in space −
akimbo, wanting, I

lack the charge. Turn
down the dwelling eye.

2 *Like Matisse*

Just as I have thought myself
into the travelling blank,
blue line, that smooth
electric shade, some bastard

in the collage-workshop
pastes on newsprint where
my head must go − *VACANCIES*
he reads, progresses *WOMEN*

on my heart, then hazards
roughly *BRIEFLY* on each breast,
across my cunt rips *SPORT*.
Puts *BUSINESS* on my arse.

3 Like Freud

On the face of it, the pearl-boned, angled
hip's no more than a body's easy warp,
a natured languor, posed indifference
in a waxy daylight. Her umbered arm
might dangle, dally on a crumpled sheet
for hours, as though she were alone. As if
the buckled, crooked leg did not occlude
the glare, throw shadow where her legs fork. Cut

under this a knowledge of my nerve-wracked,
knuckled torso, the blood-full yoke of muscle
which binds my neck, my face away from where
a brush-tip's kiss might blight my open eyes.

4 Like Sherman

That dream you have, the one where you're naked, and lying
stretched out in the back of your car, embarrassed but bold
as your friend takes the wheel. Are you drunk? You remember,
you think, just passing a woman, a suitcase and lake
where you stop for a beer at the bar and she's staring –
the woman – in close-up – in colour. She speaks as she
looks but all you can think of is hiding, and phoning
your wife, who is waiting. Waiting for change, you kill
the jump-cut, freeze-frame image you have of her laughing,
return to the bar where she's sitting to eat. You eat,
but the food is disgusting, decaying – she's making
a scene: she's crawling, you're crawling, the floor is dirt
where you're digging. You're naked. I am wearing that dream.

Drive

1 *Simply Said*

His simple is
in how a spider does

in air, work, but
leaving no stickier

trace – that is,
not even to catch

the metaphorical
fly – will *will*

the uprush of
his hourly idea,

(the one he's certain
of and dreaming),

until his tongue
clucks *You...*,

the work of it
delight and luck,

for this is Billy
talking with his heart,

saying
You. Blue car. Drive.

2 *Said So*

It was under him then, the tar lick
with its slip of miles. Too, the looped
hour, the only map he knew. To this

becoming light was where, as morning
greased it all, he went, followed
the coast road to a pebbled stop

and water, the butt of cool air
shining in his lungs. What colour is
it? *Peacock.* The day it is? *Tomorrow.*

3 Says Who?

Let's say I'm in the quiet bar as usual,
thinking the usual nothing, and the beer,

if you like, is amber. The light is, too.
Well. What happens is, I want to do

what he does: want to play the monkey
with the eye I've caught, mirror that

sad/ stupid/ happy face – show I've learnt
the language for it: body language for cabbage.

4 Sooth

If ever
this unrolling,
reeling, handsprung
wave

or man
did go, *did*
or could leave
mark – you

might say
it was in that
hard black
pebble,

the eye
of anemone, or
fingerprints
of starfish;

in the way
you thought
a man had somehow
touched

and claimed
the dark rock
at the bottom of
the pool.

Gwyneth Lewis

TIM BRETT

Selection from: *Parables & Faxes* (1995) and *Zero Gravity* (1998).

GWYNETH LEWIS writes in both Welsh, her first language, and in English, and is often concerned with dualities, enacting their interplay through the precarious balancing act of the poem (life and death, religious and secular, experience and imagination), and using the form of extended sequences to dramatise their influence on our lives.

Her poems are 'humane' (Peter Porter); 'outrageously imaginative' (Gillian Clarke); 'felicitous, urbane, heartbreaking' (Joseph Brodsky); 'full of mysteries, some of them divine, a shimmering originality, all reined in by her command of form and by a tough, demanding intelligence' (Maura Dooley). ●

Gwyneth Lewis writes:

Being bilingual, I'm very aware that there are always at least two ways of saying anything. My sequence *Parables & Faxes* was a way of exploring this in one language. *Faxes* were poems using my own direct experiences to describe the world – a lyric persona called 'I' – while *parables* employed stories from history to do the same (the three poems in this selection are all parables). I wanted to see which strand of writing would win out. In the end, I found that both were enjoyable but still incomplete ways of conveying reality. One nil to the world!

Zero Gravity came about because my cousin, Joe Tanner, was one of the astronauts who flew in the Space Shuttle on a mission to repair the Hubble Space Telescope in 1997. We went to the Shuttle launch in Florida, and had a week-long beach party while he was up in space. At the same time my husband's sister was dying of cancer, so I began to think about the similarities between their dangerous but important journeys. We saw the Hale-Bopp comet clearly in Wales, and that made me think about other internal voyages, including love, and how this life only happens once.

Of course, the language adventure is just as vertiginous for a poet as space flight is for an astronaut. Being bilingual makes you pay attention to the silence around words. You know that words are communities, habitable places, but that if you want to see the most extraordinary things, you have to don your oxygen pack and head for the black.

from Parable and Faxes

VII *Oxford Booklicker*

So the Lord said: 'Eat this scroll.'
I did and it was sweet and light and warm
and filled my belly. But I didn't speak
for all His urgings. Tolstoy's good
and Kafka nourishing. I lick

the fat from all the books I can
in the shops at lunchtime – Ovid, Byron, Keats....
The assistants know me, but they let me feast
on spaghetti sentences if I don't break the spines
of paperbacks and I replace them fast

so buyers never know their books
are licked of God. I am voracious
for the Word – a lexicon is wine
to me and wafer, so that home, at night,
I ruminate on all that's mine

inside these messages. I am the fruit
of God's expressiveness to man.
I grow on libraries, suck the grapes
of Os and uncials and still –
no prophecies. When I am ripe

I shall know and then you'll see the caravans,
processions, fleets, parades come from my mouth
as I spew up cities, colonies of words
and flocks of sentences with full-stop birds
and then, when I'm empty I shall open wide

and out will come fountains for the chosen few
to bathe in as time falls into brilliant pools,
translucent and ruined. Meantime I shall grow
stony with knowing, and my granite tongue
shall thirst (God's gargoyle!) for these blessings' blows.

XXI

And this, too, is love:

The tanker *Cliona* on the Coral Sea,
called in to assist a hospital ship
hit by the Japs and sinking in flames.
The tanker, which carries a cargo of fuel
so flammable hammers are banned on deck,
for fear their sparks might ignite stray gas,
draws near to the liner. Nurses drop down
and patients are winched from the burning hulk
to the *Cliona*, which is carrying death
but Captain O'Hara holds the ship near
to its ultimate danger and the searing heat
blisters their faces – love's garment is pain
and impossible daring. Now the undertow
brings them still closer, the whole crew burns
in anticipation of the moment she blows
and still she doesn't – how long can she last
before physical logic remembers the load –
each moment's precious, lent from the blast –
before love and its opposite crash and explode?

XXIV *Chernobyl Icon*

I saw a vision:
In a place called Pripyat
something exploded
from inside a tomb.
In the next room
someone was washing
as the geigers roared
and despite their scourging
the showers' rods
failed to restore
innocence
to the reactor's core.

The fire spread
and the roof tops burned
to show where a bride
and her nuclear groom
turned water to wormwood
while men in lead
joined in the dancing,
already dead.

And there, beyond the reactor's walls,
where Judas has hung himself,
Christ explodes
pointing a finger
as the isotopes
massacre children
on the vision's slopes.

And further out
Elijah's birds
feed him with darkness
by the motorway
and men are turned black
by the light of day.

And then, even further,
at the edge of time
Christ is baptised
in a gentle stream
and fish come to nibble,
the stars to see
God become one
with the burning flesh
that falls from men's bones
at the blinding flash

of his slightest appearance,
so the saints come to watch,
their haloes like moons,
burning like sixty thousand moons.

from **Zero Gravity**

VI

Last suppers, I fancy, are always wide-screen.
I see this one in snapshot: your brothers are rhymes
with you and each other. John has a shiner
from surfing. Already we've started counting time
backwards to zero. The Shuttle processed
out like an idol to its pagan pad.
It stands by its scaffold, being tended and blessed
by priestly technicians. You refuse to feel sad,
can't wait for your coming wedding with speed
out into weightlessness. We watch you dress
in your orange space suit, a Hindu bride,
with wires like henna for your loveliness.
You carry your helmet like a severed head.
We think of you as already dead.

III

It looks like she's drowning
in a linen tide.
They bring babies like cameras
to her bedside

because they can't see dying.
She looks too well
to be leaving. She listens
to anecdotes we tell –

how we met and got married.
She recounts a story:
her friend went stark mad
carrying, feeding, bleeding – all three

at once. She tried to bury
herself in Barry Island sand.
Her prayer plant has flowered
after seven years. She sends

Robert to fetch it from System St.
She thinks a bee sting
started the cancer.
We can't say a thing.

VIII

Thousands arrive when a bird's about to fly,
crowding the causeways. 'Houston. Weather is a go
and counting.' I pray for you as you lie
on your back facing upwards. A placard shows
local, Shuttle and universal time.
Numbers run out. Zero always comes.
'Main engines are gimballed' and I'm
not ready for this, but clouds of steam
billow out sideways and a sudden spark
lifts the rocket on a collective roar
that comes from inside us. With a sonic crack
the spaceship explodes to a flower of fire
on the scaffold's stamen. We sob and swear,
helpless, but we're lifting a sun
with our love's attention, we hear
the Shuttle's death rattle as it overcomes
its own weight with glory, setting car alarms
off in the Keys and then it's gone
out of this time zone, into the calm
of black and we've lost the lemon dawn
your vanishing made. At the viewing site
we pick oranges for your missing light.

X

Drew trips over his shadow by the pool
but picks himself up. We keep TVs on
like memorial flames, listen as Mission Control
gives cool instructions You are a sun
we follow, tracking your time over Africa,
a fauvist desert. We see you fall
past pointillist clouds in the Bahamas,
past glaciers, silent hurricanes, the Nile.

We're all provincials when it comes to maps
so we look out for Florida. The world's a road
above you – but you have no 'up',
only an orbit as you dive towards
an opal Pacific, now you see dawn
every ninety minutes. The Shuttle's a cliff
that's shearing, you on it, every way's 'down',
vertiginous plunging. It is yourself
you hold on to, till you lose your grip
on that, even. Then your soul's the ship.

XI

The second time the comet swung by
the knife went deeper. It hissed through the sky,

phosphorus on water. It marked a now,
an only-coming-once, a this-ness we knew

we'd keep forgetting. Its vapour trails
mimicked our voyage along ourselves,

our fire with each other, the endless cold
which surrounds that burning. Don't be fooled

by fireworks. It's no accident that *leave*
fails but still tries to rhyme with *love*.

XIII

What is her vanishing point?
Now that she's dead
but still close by
we assume she's heard

our conversations.
Out of sight? Out of mind?
On her inward journey
she's travelled beyond

the weight of remembering.
The g-force lifts
from her labouring chest.
Forgetting's a gift

of lightness. She's sped
vast distances
already, she's shed
her many bodies –

cancer, hope, regard,
marriage, forgiving.
Get rid of time
and everything's dancing,

forget straight lines,
all's blown away.
Now's honey from the bees of night,
music from the bees of day.

XIV

There are great advantages to having been dead.
They say that Lazarus never laughed again,
but I doubt it. Your space suit was a shroud
and at night you slept in a catacomb,
posed like a statue. So, having been
out to infinity, you experienced the heat
and roar of re-entry, blood in the veins
then, like a baby, had to find your feet
under you, stagger with weight, learn to cope
again with gravity. Next came the tour
of five states with a stopover in Europe.
You let people touch you, told what you saw.
This counts as a death and a second birth
within one lifetime. This point of view
is radical, its fruit must be mirth
at one's own unimportance and now, although
you're famous, a "someone", you might want much less.
Your laughter's a longing for weightlessness.

Julia Copus

TOLGA BALOGLU

JULIA COPUS's vision is remarkably mature for a young writer, with poems in her first collection encompassing the whole span of life, from birth to parenthood, betrayal, ageing and death. Her poetry is highly musical and delicately wrought. Strangely familiar characters from myth throw the turmoil of love and family relationships into sharp relief, with the child's fear of abandonment confronted in searing accounts of marital break-up. 'Her poems view some of the most turbulent moments in life through a sharp, clear lens: mature, uncomfortably honest, uncompromising' (Maura Dooley). ●

Selection from: *The Shuttered Eye* (1995) and new poems.

Julia Copus writes:

Writing poems is a bit like panning for gold. You have to be prepared to sit for a long while in the cold murk of the river-bed and grow heavy with alluvial dust for the sake of the gold it contains. A lot of the initial shaping of poems goes on subconsciously: the poet might lift a few ready phrases from pages of brainstormed scrawl, work hard at filling in the gaps, but meanwhile the poem is also hard at work, clothing itself in the rhythms and patterns that suit it best.

Two of the following poems ('The Back Seat of My Mother's Car' and 'The Clothes') have wrapped themselves in an entirely new form which I've called *specular*, where the second half unfolds mirror-like from the first, using the same lines but in reverse order. The result of this discipline should be no more mechanical than a good sonnet or fugue. Here, it echoes the way my mind remembered these two traumas at the time of writing, replaying events until the precise sequence of them became obscured.

Those poems both deal in different ways with the difficulties of familial love. But ties often need to be severed in order to gain something new, especially if you're a *sea-polyp* and you reproduce asexually, losing part of your own body to create a new being in its own right.

My advice to new writers is to work at heaping up a compost of dreams, ideas and language for their poems, accumulating words that don't quite work in order to get closer to the ones that do. A flower, after all, is just a weed that got lucky.

The Back Seat of My Mother's Car

We left before I had time
to comfort you, to tell you that we nearly touched
hands in that vacuous half-dark. I wanted
to stem the burning waters running over me like tiny
rivers down my face and legs, but at the same time I was reaching out
for the slit in the window where the sky streamed in,
cold as ether, and I could see your fat mole-fingers grasping
the dusty August air. I pressed my face to the glass;
I was calling to you – *Daddy!* – as we screeched away into
the distance, my own hand tingling like an amputation.
You were mouthing something I still remember, the noiseless words
piercing me like that catgut shriek that flew up, furious as a sunset
pouring itself out against the sky. The ensuing silence
was the one clear thing I could decipher –
the roar of the engine drowning your voice,
with the cool slick glass between us.

With the cool slick glass between us,
the roar of the engine drowning, your voice
was the one clear thing I could decipher –
pouring itself out against the sky, the ensuing silence
piercing me like that catgut shriek that flew up, furious as a sunset.
You were mouthing something: I still remember the noiseless words,
the distance, my own hand tingling like an amputation.
I was calling to you, Daddy, as we screeched away into
the dusty August air. I pressed my face to the glass,
cold as ether, and I could see your fat mole-fingers grasping
for the slit in the window where the sky streamed in
rivers down my face and legs, but at the same time I was reaching out
to stem the burning waters running over me like tiny
hands in that vacuous half-dark. I wanted
to comfort you, to tell you that we nearly touched.
We left before I had time.

The Sea-Polyp

Spineless and eyeless we spend our days
streaming circlets of tentacles
in the languid flow of the tide, effusing
grass skirts, snake-hair. To multiply we
simply divide; unknowingly and overnight
we lose a small part of ourselves
into the blueblack gloaming, deep and icily.

Often in clusters in clear deep pools
you will find us, gossamer-pink and clinging
to rocks as if we happened there: fleshy eruptions
on some dry pock-face, spreading our bases,
possessive, attached, and though we can't recreate
Medusa's stony stare, it is true that we paralyse with
the sinuous lengths of our hair; our elastic mouths
can accommodate creatures twice our size.

Lately I've been noticing, just a little
further down my rock, a new appendage – small,
bristling, perfectly formed, it has grown
a fine mouth-stalk and is relishing
independence, I think, but looks, by all accounts,
remarkably like me.

The Making of Eve

And kneeling one day at the sea's edge God
scooped a fist of mud from the earth and pressed it
into a shape called man. Its coldness spread

like an ache through his fingers and as He
stooped to warm them by chance a small
cloud of breath seeped into the shape and it lived.

But by and by when the sun was high up
in the sky man began to crack and fall
into pieces. Then God lifted some salt

water into his cupped hands and called it
woman, smoothing it into the fractured clay.
Now whenever man got hot he hankered for

a long cool sip from woman and she
assented sometimes wanting a place
to rest safe from the tireless assaults

of the wind and craving for a while
a different sort of medium to move in.

The Art of Interpretation

A plain wood table, the obligatory
vase of flowers, the writer's head bent low
over his work. At the far end, a window.

Open. Apart from this there is little
to help us with the story: the room is left
deliberately bare, inviting us

to speculate. Consider, for instance,
the window as eye. Is it looking out
or looking in? Notice, too, the dark, plum

sheen of the nib; and the pen, not poised
but resting, heavy, on the page. Unused.
Do you see how the artist plays the light

off against the shade? The candle, also,
is misleading: I advise you to ignore
the warmth of its glow. Drop the temperature

a little. Allow your eyes to wander
over the shadows, where the details are:
the clearly-labelled absinthe flask, half full,

half empty; the sweeping lines of the words
in the open letter, just visible
under the lifeless curl of his fingers.

Now turn up the volume of background noise,
the pub's detritus in the street outside.
Bring it level with the window. Then cut.

The Cricketer's Retirement Day

It seemed the obvious place to go, the sea.
And when he reached it there it was, exactly
as he had remembered it; it didn't pause
or lift its gaze but went on casually
sporting at the land's edge, kitted out
in the usual ships and birds, and blinking now and then,
as if it had itself that moment just
stepped out from some dusty pavilion.
I am no one, said the cricketer
(somewhat theatrically);
my playing days are done. And he lay down
flatly as a wave in the shade of a cove
and filled up his ears with the sound of the wind
to muffle the beating of his conscious mind.

And when he next looked up again
a mesh of rain had occupied the sky –
large drops of water disappearing softly
into the totality of water. The ships had left
the harbour and the birds were gone.
Only the waves remained there: dumb, hypnotic,
arching and falling in the fibrous light, just
arching and falling into themselves
the way a ball describes itself in flight.

Widower

I believe it was a calm evening,
when the sky was least expecting it,

the ancient volcano snapped awake
and oozed a country, which hardened, formed

per second per second through the years
to shape the landscape we scrambled through

that last summer together, searching
for the dusty chapels underground,

paintings of Christ with the eyes scratched out.
She looked so small beneath them even then.

Her first time abroad, and soon after the earth
reached up and kissed her, full on the mouth.

And now I'm here in this tea-garden
we visited – city of two

continents, they call it – I like that,
the cool water running in between.

I like the honesty of the place,
the way it speaks of uncertainty,

like these first stars twitching at the brim
of the parasol. Even the sea,

which has so much to say to us, can't
stops its lip from trembling at the shore.

The Clothes
(for Kim, 1958-1997)

They seem too pale for these cloud-breached days,
spread out on my floor now – pastels mostly,
intended for the hot Australian sky
that trembled on your skin; cool cotton prints
that languished happy over chairbacks as you slept.
These are the clothes you wore, their soft slack limbs
burdened with dreams, pining for your body, needing you
to fill them up with life. In spite of which the world goes on –
the sun that pricked your light blue eyes awake
is with us still, the hedgerows rustling with the leaves they shed
in memory of you, and that dream-soaked sky, the sea,
playing out its restless melodramas
on the coastline where you lived.
Life moves in seasons, dressing and undressing.

Life moves in seasons, dressing and undressing
on the coastline where you lived,
playing out its restless melodramas
in memory of you. And that dream-soaked sky, the sea,
is with us still, the hedgerows rustling with the leaves they shed,
the sun that pricked your light blue eyes awake
to fill them up with life. In spite of which the world goes on,
burdened with dreams, pining for your body, needing you.
These are the clothes you wore, their soft slack limbs,
that languished happy over chairbacks as you slept,
that trembled on your skin; cool cotton prints
intended for the hot Australian sky.
Spread out on my floor now, pastels mostly,
they seem too pale for these cloud-breached days.

Eleanor Brown

Selection from: *Maiden Speech* (1996) and new work.

ELEANOR BROWN writes powerfully of love, and hilariously of love's pitfalls. She works as a barmaid, observing the kind of 'enjoyable juxtapositions' which Maura Dooley admires in 'this witty sophisticated writer who handles rhythm and rhyme, the men and the boys, with equal assurance'. Her *Fifty Sonnets*, 'a subtly sustained and cunningly crafted sonnet sequence, assessing an affair, comprises the last rites it abjures' (Stewart Conn). 'She displays the sharp wit of a Molière, with graceful, cerebral rhymes that leave a bitter aftertaste. Ever insightful and enormously funny, she juxtaposes moving descriptions with killer punch-lines' (*Time Out*). ●

Eleanor Brown writes:

Sonnet sequences are what I recommend as reading matter for anyone who is working split shifts. They can be picked up and put down in moments, and you don't need to worry about losing your place or a narrative thread.

You have time to commit a sonnet to memory in your afternoon break, notoriously too short to go home and do anything useful, like sleep. At the very least, a good closing couplet will hang around and be poignant in your head throughout the long evening stretch of your shift, while you ask people if they want garlic bread with that ('I, cumbred with good manners, answer do, / But know not how. For still I think of you'). After a while, you may find that your two and half hours' time off is just enough to go to a café and compose a sonnet yourself; this is not altogether a bad thing, as it keeps you off the streets and out of idle conversation. Longer stretches of leisure may lead to experimentation with poems of more than fourteen lines. An excess of leisure gives rise to dreadfully long poems, and total unemployment can cause novels.

In my experience, café proprietors do not accept sonnets in lieu of payment, so unless you are very winsome, you should take care to earn enough in lunchtime tips to buy a cup of coffee, and make it last. Finally, if anyone bothers you with questions about what you are reading or writing, tell them, and they will be sure to leave you in peace.

Bitcherel

You ask what I think of your new acquisition;
and since we are now to be 'friends',
I'll strive to the full to cement my position
with honesty. Dear – it depends.

It depends upon taste, which must not be disputed;
for which of us *does* understand
why some like their furnishings pallid and muted,
their cookery wholesome, but bland?

There isn't a *law* that a face should have features,
it's just that they generally *do*;
God couldn't give colour to *all* of his creatures,
and only gave wit to a few;

I'm sure she has qualities, much underrated,
that compensate amply for this,
along with a charm that is so understated
it's easy for people to miss.

And if there are some who choose clothing to flatter
what beauties they think they possess,
when what's underneath has no shape, does it matter
if there is no shape to the dress?

It's not that I think she is *boring*, precisely,
that isn't the word I would choose;
I know there are men who like girls who talk nicely
and always wear sensible shoes.

It's not that I think she is vapid and silly;
it's not that her voice makes me wince;
but – chilli con carne without any chilli
is only a plateful of mince...

from **Fifty Sonnets**

VIII

Probably the most human thing I do,
apart from dancing; and the only time
I'm not engaged in finding words for you,
or for myself, or fishing for a rhyme.
'The perfect sexual experience'?
Perhaps you misinterpret my ideal;
ecstasy, angel choirs, no preference
of mine: the act, ridiculous and real.
    In retrospect, that first, unfortunate
and technically disastrous time, when we
were stripped of glamour, robbed of dignity –
my giggling fit, and the importunate
telephone, and your three-times-lost erection:
that time, perhaps, was closest to perfection.

XI

Tell me I'm beautiful, and bring me flowers.
Tell me I'm fascinating, and you've never
met anyone so witty or so clever.
Worship me; sit and think of me for hours;
speak me the language of idolatry.
Go off your food. Fall sick. Have sleepless nights.
Resign your freedom, and all other rights.
Be bored without me. Write me poetry.
Don't notice other women; or compare
them with me, in my favour, if you do.
Earnestly tell me I'm too good for you.
Tell me you love me. Love me. Tell me there
is nothing you would not do for my sake.
These, and other demands, I do not make.

XXIII

What do I have, when I contemplate this,
more than the knowledge that something has passed?
Something untruthful and warm as your kiss;
brilliant, brief, and too lawless to last;
free as gratuitous violence, and
serious, laughing and dark as your eyes;
rare as your compliments, deft as your hand;
highly desirable, highly unwise;
something that summoned me out of my state
(where I was happy) of being alone;
something that happened too soon or too late,
yes – but it happened. And it is my own.
What do I have? This intangible stuff.
Little enough – but though little, enough.

XL

When I recall you – as I often do –
between two paragraphs, against my will
(I try to keep you in parentheses,
but you will interrupt my reading as
you did my careful life, appearing through
the ruptured print to laugh at it), I still
hold the book open; part of me still sees
the page; but all my concentration has
swarmed to the memory of moments when
we sat and talked in other company;
and through a comment, every now and then,
the sudden, private glance you cut to me,
the flicker of amusement in your brow,
shredded my gravity, and shreds me now.

Beauty and the Prince Formerly Known as Beast

He likes to do the kind of thing that shows
his fine hands to advantage, when he knows

he's being watched. He paints on silk; he plays
the harpsichord or lute, although his gaze

is always on his polished fingernails;
when meals are ended, now, he never fails

to glance around the dining-table, shoot
his cuffs, select and peel a piece of fruit

with elegant dexterity...discards
it, after, and suggests a game of cards.

The fashion is for shaving very close,
and unplucked eyebrows are considered gross.

Men wear their hair tied neatly back, or short.
Hunting is rather frowned upon, at court,

though there has been a certain renaissance
in verse, theatricals and formal dance.

He dances consummately well. We make
a lovely-looking couple, when we take

the polished floor together. Later on,
the thousand candles snuffed, the guests all gone,

he'll take my hand in his, apply a slight
pressure with his cool lips, and say goodnight.

Then I remember how he looked at me
under that curse, when I would go to bed,
deep-set eyes burning in his shaggy head –
he used to look at me quite hungrily.

With this most gentle of all gentlemen,
it would be wrong to ask for that again;

I don't. But on my own, some nights at least,
I lie and wish, a little, for my Beast.

Jezebel to the Eunuchs

No priests. No tiring-women. If you please,
no pity, though I don't object to fear.
Furthermore, absolutely no
prophets, croaking 'I told you so.'
Lock up this turret room; give me the keys.
Vengeance can bloody come and get me here.
No prayers, reproaches, tears or homilies.
You three are privileged, you realise?
Marred men, whom nobody can mend,
you'll see how greatness makes its end –
even take part. You place your sympathies
where you want to; your Queen accepts she dies
in any case. You see that cloud of dust?
That's Jehu, driving like a lunatic.
Poor, god-pecked Jehu, comes to close
my wicked mouth for good. Ah, those
Jews, majestic tools of Yahweh! It must –
I can't believe it doesn't ever stick
in their throats, to grovel for such a god.
Pathetically obsessed with cleanliness,
their god. Well, just in case I meet
him: perfumed oil, to make me sweet
(no time for a bath now). You think this odd?
You'd dress for dinner, but you wouldn't dress
for death? I'll be prepared. Rouge, now, and kohl.
That smaller brush. Death: the greatest and last
of any woman's appointments –
surely the usual ointments
are not out of place – she should stay in rôle,
for fear of seeming to regret her past.

All past, the 'whoredoms, witchcrafts', sins and snares,
abominable to God. Or so they tell
me. Is he here yet? At the gate?
Oh, Jehu, Jehu – just too late.
Vengeance, that thinks to take me unawares
finds me ready, and looking...rather well.

All the Little Mermaids

Prepare to be slapped with the fact of your
own ordinariness. She won't look up
from what she's knitting, or her dirty cup;
your taut face won't intrigue her any more
than any of the others. *Well, which is it?*
Something you can't live with, or something you
can't live without? she'll ask, knit one purl two
knit one, *Or is this just a social visit?*

She won't be listening while you explain
the intricate predicament – she'll wait
for your stammering halt, then indicate
a dog-eared price-list. You will pay. *The pain,*
she'll say, *is sharp at first, but you can learn*
how to seem unaffected. There will be
no anaesthetic, and no guarantee.
For me, it was soon over: a thin burn,

a thread of fire she fed into my throat
to hook the voice out. Afterwards I bled
a little, and it hurt to turn my head
in order not to look at it, afloat
in a cracked basin. Outside, the old wives
muttered and nudged each other as I passed –
she's not the first, and she won't be the last,
because I walked as though I walked on knives.

Tracey Herd

MOIRA CONWAY

Selection from: *No Hiding Place* (1996) and new poems.

TRACEY HERD is a Scottish poet whose dark poems draw on detective stories and *film noir* – with their battles between good and evil – as well as the contemporary world of Hollywood, racing and supermodels. For her heroines – Ophelia or Monroe, murder or fashion victims – there is no hiding place from death, God and the judgement of others. 'Tracey Herd's strange personal iconography becomes steadily more charged and disturbing as these obsessive, darkly sexual poems accumulate. Terrible chasms seem to lurk beneath even the most innocently domestic of her subjects. These poems clearly compelled themselves to be written' (Don Paterson). ●

Tracey Herd writes:

History, childhood and horses are my three main obsessions. 'The Survivors' and 'The Bathing Girls' are poems of childhood – the dark side and the hopeful side. 'Coronach' was written for a colleague who died in a climbing accident; *coronach* is Gaelic for a lament but is also the name of the 1926 Derby winner. 'Hyperion's Bones' is about the 1933 Derby winner whose remains were found in a tea chest in a garden shed and reassembled to stand in the National Horse Racing Museum at Newmarket. Someone once asked me why I always wrote about dead horses, and I had to explain that I was interested in the history of horse racing and dead horses themselves didn't excite me. I did write a poem about Sir Ivor when he was gambolling happily in retirement but three weeks later I opened the *Sporting Life* to be greeted by the headline 'Sir Ivor Dies', which made me feel inexplicably guilty.

I'm fascinated by female icons, as in 'Marilyn Climbs Out of the Pool' and 'The Pink Rose Rings', which tries to capture and freeze the split second of Kennedy's assassination through the mind of his wife Jacqueline. Jackie Kennedy and Marilyn make brief reappearances in later work, as does Rita Hayworth in 'Bombshell' – the blurred blonde of 'Marilyn Climbs Out of the Pool' is now an incandescent redhead thrown into sharp relief by the blinding explosion of the atom bomb, not merely by photographers' flash-bulbs. I'm working on a long sequence with a Nancy Drew type heroine who is forced to confront a century which has pretty much passed her by – more female icons here.

The Survivors

I came at night to the dark house
where the father had taken the fuse
from the fuse-box and killed the lights.

I came at night when the weepy mother sat
doll-like in the front room, cross-legged on the carpet,
hands stinging from smacking the brats,

listening to crackly recordings of Glenn Miller,
her heels drumming on the well-worn floor:
the plane crash had wiped her mind out.

The thumb-sized father climbed the stairs
with a candle, searching for survivors.

The Bathing Girls

Lighting her thin French cigarette
with a flaring match, flinging her head
back to exhale her looping signature
in smoke, she plucked April's *Vogue*
from her smart red corduroy satchel.

She wet her thumb and peeled
the cover back. Sunlight fell
on an interior pungent and dazzling
as freshly painted walls. I breathed
deeply and took the plunge.

Six bathing girls in strapless suits
linked arms and ran out from a cerulean
ocean, their ankles fluted columns
tilting through the waves.
I hugged my school books close

not wanting to see how my friend's sweater
clung to her tiny breasts, but unable
to take my eyes from her slicked red mouth.
I wanted to lean forward and kiss her.
In those days, anything seemed possible.

The Pink Rose Rings

She remembered seeing the underpass up ahead
and thinking how cool it would be when they slipped
into its shade. That was mere seconds before his hands
flew to the black hole in his throat. She turned
then, dazzled, the sun seeming to explode
beside her in the car. She remembered
the intricate pink rose rings in his skull, vivid
as the flowers that lay beside them on the seat,
and cradling his head, bewildered by the riot
of colour, wilting a little in the unseasonable heat.

Coronach

The skylark's melody is sealed in ice:
a coronach as blue as the winter
sky. The moon wobbles over the rock face,
throwing into high relief the climber
in a gully below the glittering maze.

He is a brilliant figure in this frieze.
His genius walked him into space
and left him to find a foothold there.
The moon is sheer ice or a cracked watch-face
that swings on its fragile chain of stars.

Night is falling at its own modest pace.

Marilyn Climbs Out of the Pool

He made her do the same scene
fifty times. Flashbulbs
light up her face
as she slips in and out
of the water with barely
a wrinkle of blue.

The cameras light up the pool
like bursts of applause.
Again and again she smiles
making hard work of it all,
bringing one glistening limb
right out of the water.
Her toes reach for the concrete edge:
her fair hair curls damply
over one bare shoulder.
Her eyes are the colour of the water,
night blue with silver
darting frantically in every direction.

Hyperion's Bones

In a garden shed two tea-chests
gave their treasure protection
from the light and whipping draughts.

No ordinary bones, the caption
reads, beneath the intricate
resurrection of your skeleton:

once *a glowing chestnut with four white
fetlocks*, barely larger than a pony,
but *deep through the chest*,

who swept past giants to win his Derby
and was named for a god.
There is something lacking in the rigid display:

the carriage of that handsome head
is stiff, not *extraordinarily proud.*
Common sense says the spirit's fled

the tea-chests and the garden shed
sneezed out from its dusty bones.
On a windswept Heath, the ghosts are on parade.

All May, the rain's drummed down
loud as hoofbeats on your old training ground.
The weather clears in June.

The final furlong sees the sun strike gold,
distancing itself with contemptuous ease
from the chasing pack of black clouds.

Bombshell

The red-headed G.I.'s favourite
unpins her elaborate waves;
a scarlet carnage, the mind's

debacle. She discards
the metal clips on her dresser.
Her hairline was raised

fractionally, by electrolysis
leaving the high forehead
taut, shining.

It was painful and slow
but she bore it patiently.
Her eyebrows were plucked

almost to extinction
then arched and shaded in
like history rewritten.

She is radiant, her smile
flaring over the white sands,
the blue, boiling ocean.

from The Mystery of the Missing Century

* * * *

I stopped the car and stepped out onto gravel,
careful to grab my bag and lock the door.
I paused for half a minute to admire
the huge, overgrown gardens, the marble

statues, toppled or cracked or discoloured,
the woman who held a finger to her broken mouth
as if that might stop the secrets on her breath
from spilling out like leaves or water. I stopped,

I think, for more than half a minute.
I held my own breath, as somewhere a door
creaked open, then slammed shut like thunder.
I paused, out of caution, not fear, but my heart

took off at a gallop, my titian hair
streaming wildly in the wind which began
to rustle in the trees and soon outran
my heart which quietened down. I never

lost control in any situation: rule number one
and probably the most important one.

* * * *

We are sailing on a charming bay,
all blue and gold and spilling
light. Bess leans back, lazily trailing
one hand through the fan-tailed spray

giggling at her distorted reflection.
I have a picture in my head,
another Bess, blonde, sweet and scared,
shivering as she crouches down

in an alley at the back of Hollywood.
The photographer stalks her
through the trash until she murmurs,
that's enough, goes back to bed.

The hidden bell will toll to warn
of water rising in the cave.
My pulse will quicken with each wave
as my sharp eyes swiftly scan

the darkness for a phantom, any phantom,
or the blank-faced drowning woman.
I no longer have the golden lines:
she'll have to save herself this time.

The blonde scrubs her face until it stings.
The photographer nervously hovers
wanting a caption for his pictures.
Call them the end of everything.

Katrina Porteous

Selection from: *The Lost Music* (1996).

KATRINA PORTEOUS celebrates her love of the Northumberland village of Beadnell, the place and its people. In a dialogue between her own voice and the dialect of the fishermen, she traces the identity of her community in its common memory and working practices, finding with the passing of the old ways of life a loss of spiritual direction. 'There is throughout an engagement with process – be it of natural growth and decay or of human love and mourning – that demands prolonged patience, careful observation and unwavering purpose. A rage for order informs the fashioning of these cadences which resonate in the memory' (Stephen Romer). ●

Katrina Porteous writes:

I write about the things around me: in particular, change. Northumberland's coastal villages, once centred upon the inshore fishing industry, are changing rapidly. Aware of this, I worked very closely with local fishermen over several years, immersing myself in their vanishing way of life. Old men like Charlie Douglas were natural conservationists, wanting to pass on their livelihood to future generations. They held in their memories an inherited map of the sea-floor and its stories that no technology could replace.

Fishing is for me a microcosm, embodying many themes which concern me: the continuity between the human and the natural worlds, and the importance of memory in shaping our present and future identity. So much in contemporary life breaks this continuity between past and future, individual and community, and estranges us from nature and ourselves.

Poetry matters because it strives for truth and does so through love. It finds the spiritual, the eternal, in the ordinary, physical world. It is very important to me that my poems should be accessible to all, and memorable. For this reason I often use rhyme. I use Northumbrian dialect, too – not always comprehensible in its literal sense, but utterly accessible in its sounds. My title *The Lost Music* reflects my belief in a hidden order underlying the surface chaos of life. Poetry is closer to music than to other written forms; because its rhythms, and the sounds words make, are directly expressive of feeling, it needs to be read out loud. It was a great privilege to work with men like Charlie, whose dialect was particularly rich in expressive sounds.

Calf

Outside my window a cow is giving birth.
Wrapped up in plastic, the calf dives feet-first
Onto the rain-sodden, trampled turf.

And at once it is desperate to be upright;
Heaves, flops, kicks as if sky was its birthright,
And not even the sudden slide from dark into daylight

Tugs like the gravity that drags it back to earth.

I Envy the Cracked, Black Basalt

I envy the cracked, black basalt
Its incontrovertible form,
Fixed to resist the slow, sweet erosion
Of ocean and storm.

And the sea-swallow I envy for his lightness
And his leaving without the least look back,
And his pure, unmerciful, sky-high, ecstatic
Attack.

And I envy his roost, where the wind, tides and river
Contend to release
At last, from long battle, a landscape of absolute
Stillness, and peace.

And I envy the limpet his small, hard hold
Under wave after wave of blind water, his not letting go;
And I envy the sand,
That it slips through the cracks in the fastness of basalt,

And flows.

Charlie Douglas

'We're gan' tyek hor off, th' morn,'
Said Charlie, squatting in his black-tarred hut;
And the other old fishermen muttered, spat, swore.
So after a thin night, cracked by storm,
I arrived by the harbour kilns at dawn,
Where the sour *Jane Douglas* smoked and heaved,
Rocking her burden of dans and creeves.
And Charlie, a tab in his toothless jaw,
Stared blindly out to Featherblaa',
Tiller in hand. And away she roared,
Her proud bows rising, blue and white,
The same cold colours as the changing light
Bowling over the wind-torn sea.
Now, all the creatures that creep below,
Lobster and nancy, crab and frone,
From many million years ago
Have secret places, and Charlie knows
The banks and hollows of every part.
He's learnt their lineaments by heart
And mapped the landscape beneath the sea.
O, I was the blind man then, not he.
Now Charlie's quiet. His words were few:
'Aah'll tell ye somethin'. Now this is true –
We're finished, hinny. The fishin's deed.
Them greet, muckle traa'lers – it's nowt but greed.
Whae, there's nae bloody chance for the fish t' breed...
An' the lobsters! Y' bugger! In wor day
W' hoyed aa' th' berried hens away!'
'And they don't do that now?' 'Darsay noo!'
As he spoke, I watched the steeple grow
Smaller, still smaller, marking where
His folk, for the last three-hundred years,
Were christened and married and laid to rest.
So I urged him to tell me of all the past,
That other, hidden, deep-sea floor;
And whatever I'd cherished in life before –
Home, friends – just then, I loved him more,
This crined old man of eighty-two;

I wanted to trawl him through and through
For all the mysteries he knew
About the sea, about the years.
I wanted to haul his memories free
Like a string of creeves from the troubled sea,
Shining with swad and water-beads.
But turning his fierce, blind gaze on me,
His eyes said, 'Hinny, ye'll nivvor see –
Ye divvin't tell them aa' ye kna
Or aal your stories in a day.'

dans: marker buoys; *creeves:* crab or lobster pots; *nancy:* squat lobster;
frone: starfish; *berried hens:* female lobsters carrying eggs; *swad:* the green,
fringed seaweed that clings to ropes.

Decommissioning

They are burning a boat on the beach.
Grim-backed, they watch
In a darkness that crackles with fear.

Their faces leap up through the flames,
Masks hacked out of wood,
Reeling, red as blood,
Round the funeral pyre on the sand.

The planks sunder and peel
Like the great black ribs of a whale.
Unclenched, they fall,

And the sparks stream away on the wind,
And they sting like spray, smart
Like the ice-driven spray of winter
That burns in the dark –

An ache they would understand
And suffer more easily
Than the small white scrap of paper

Whose vacancy
Tells what the landsman knows
Of a boat and its burden.
Charlie, Jack, Stephen:

They slip away through the smoke,
So many nails wrenched free,
Unfastened from the sea.

Wrecked Creeves

When I see lobster pots the sea has mangled,
The bow-sticks smashed like ribs, the covers tangled
Like wild hair round the lats, the strops all frayed,
It's not the wasting sea I think of, but the men who made them.

Whose hedge-knife stripped these ash sticks in the plantin?
His sea-boot bent each bow till, green and pliant,
Its arch sprang in his arms. Whose fingers, weaving
Strong knots, braided this net one firelit evening?

He hammered home the wedges, and his arm
Beat like a blacksmith's on the stubborn frame;
Deft, then, he intricately stitched inside
With a surgeon's delicacy and a master's eye.

Last week I found a plank stamped R.D.B.
He's dead. But Robbie's creeves still fish this sea
For other men, till east winds and spring tides
Return his broken sticks to the countryside.

There, on the live green grass above the beach,
They're strewn like human bones, worm-riddled, bleached;
And in the warm noon sunshine, bright with larks,
They say, 'Yon sea is caa'd, an' aa'ful dark.'

lats: cross-wise planks on pot's base; *strops:* ropes attached to pots;
plantin: plantation.

Roddy Lumsden

MOIRA CONWAY

Selection from: *Yeah Yeah Yeah* (1997) and *The Book of Love* (2000).

RODDY LUMSDEN's poems eavesdrop on a half urban, half surreal world of lovers and losers trying on roles and acting out fantasies. Their sly self-mockery and playful, blustering tone recall the twilight dislocations between pub and bedroom of someone who once made his living at night by playing quiz machines and working as a quizmaster (and now writes newspaper puzzles). His poems, says Alan Warner, are 'full of intellectual marauding ...This is the poetic world of male guilt, of a smoker, of a Villonesque drinker, a 3am rolling Homer with an attendant and vicious intelligence...all we can ask for in poetry: contemplation, intelligence, stylistic beauty.' ●

Roddy Lumsden writes:

Summarising my work is a parlour game, but I should say that I'm a formalist, interested in the arcana of human nature, sex, music and names, concerned with surface as much as depth. Many pieces are first person, character narratives – I hope readers will listen to the narrator and then consider why I chose that dummy for my ventriloquism. The idea of the poetic persona is attractive to me. I am prolific and protean: qualities which have their drawbacks. Though I'm happy to be Scottish, I'm not 'a Scottish poet'. I'm a "scene" poet, in that I attend readings, teach, review, organise and host events and actually buy and read lots of contemporary poetry.

Of the poems here, 'Yeah Yeah Yeah' is one of my 'Sonnets of the Unexpected', twisting The Beatles' 'She Loves You'. A set-piece poem like that writes itself. 'Mercy' has been over-praised: a true story I heard in a pub to which I added rhymes. People like its morbidity, so I still read it out, like Mud doing 'Tiger Feet' for the eight-thousandth time. The couple have since split up. 'Show and Tell' was the product of a grim morning when I was ill (much of *The Book of Love* was written during illness and it shows in a bittersweet way). 'Tricks for the Barmaid' set off from an obscure song-lyric into self-referential mockery (I write *The Scotsman*'s Brain Game puzzles). 'ITMA' (*It's That Man Again*, a wartime radio comedy) was written after the writer Paul Reekie taped *Silly Songs of the 20s and 30s* for me; humour was coarse between the wars. It's also a dig at the intellectualisation of the punk ethos.

Then

For the first time, I listen to a lost
and secret recording of us
making love near-on ten years ago.

I recognise your voice, your sounds,
though if I knew no better,
I could be any man in any room.

After, the rising sounds of rising
and of dressing and once
as you step up close to the deck,

perhaps to pick up shoes, you sing
the chorus of *Sunday Morning*.
I call on you to hurry and we leave.

It does not end then; the tape rolls on.
A few late cars which sigh by
might have passed us walking away

triumphant, unaware we've left behind
this mop and mow mechanism
of silence to which we may never return.

Yeah Yeah Yeah

No matter what you did to her, she said,
There's times, she said, she misses you, your face
Will pucker in her dream, and times the bed's
Too big. Stray hairs will surface in a place
You used to leave your shoes. A certain phrase,
Some old song on the radio, a joke
You had to be there for, she said, some days
It really gets to her; the way you smoked
Or held a cup, or her, and how you woke
Up crying in the night sometimes, the way

She'd stroke and hush you back, and how you broke
Her still. All this she told me yesterday,
Then she rolled over, laughed, began to do
To me what she so rarely did with you.

Prayer To Be with Mercurial Women

Let me never have her father
call me, saying how's about
a round of golf? Instead I'll take
the grim, forbidding monster
who inspects me for a crooked
trouser crease. And spare me too
from palmy evenings which sail by
in restaurants, on barstools,
without a storming off or two.
'Darling, you were made for me.'
I pray I'll never hear those words.
I need to feel I'm stealing
love another man would kill for.
When in sleep she curls herself
around me, may she whisper names
that are not mine. I'd prefer
to be the second best she's had.
A curse on mouths which dovetail
as if there'd been a blueprint made:
I'd rather blush and slobber.
And once a month, please let me be
a punchbag. I'll take the blame
for everything: I want to taste
the stinging of a good slap.
I hope I'll find my begging notes
crumpled, torn in half, unread,
and when I phone, I want to hear
an endless sound of ringing.
Help me avoid the kind of girl
who means things when she says them,
unless she's screeching, telling me
exactly what I am. Amen.

Mercy

And so, on my return, the terrapins,
Two upturned ashtrays farced with viscera,
Are scrabbling at the bathtub's side, par-boiled
And livid, haggling with mortality –
You having gamely carried out your chore,
Though muddling the hot tap and the cold.

Some skin flakes off. We wait a week before
The first succumbs, breaks water belly-up.
Next morning, you are sent to check the tank.
The second peels and pines, pricks you with guilt.
I scour the owner's manual for hints
On mercy killing methods, come up blank.

This calls for some imagination, since,
Too big to flush away, too still alive
For burial, tradition lets us down.
I scoop it out and drop it in a sack,
While you slip out to start the car, and soon
We're driving slowly to the edge of town.

We circle, find a quiet spot – the moon
A single, silent witness to the deed.
It flails, a wriggling terror in my lap.
I settle it shell-up beneath a tyre;
You deftly hold a balance on the clutch,
Accelerate. I listen for the snap.

At first, it won't appear to matter much;
We'll dine out on the story more than once.
The new pair looks much like the tragic one
And, when you tape those labels, Life and Death,
Onto the bath-taps, how we'll stand and laugh,
Though something sharp will snag us, later on.

Tricks for the Barmaid

'*None of us are the Waltons*, Ricki Lake said that,'
I tell her, as she shuffles piles of change.

'Did you know most 1950s ice cream vans
played *The Happy Wanderer*?' She blanks me.

'Elvis's last words were *OK, I won't*.' 'And when
will I hear yours?' she asks. We're getting somewhere now.

I do that burning matchstick trick, you know the one.
She polishes the brass taps with a yellow cloth.

I point out *cappucino* should have double c.
She chalks it in without a second glance at me.

I show my double-jointed fingers, roll my tongue
and puff my cheeks out till they're red and hold my breath

for several minutes. She tips a Smirnoff bottle up
and clips it to the optic. I know all the words

to *Baker Street* and prove it to her. She knocks off
The Scotsman Brain Game puzzle, starts to yawn.

I tell her, 'It's a long day for the devil, love.'
And it's only then I know who she reminds me of:

it's not that girl I saw in a crowd once but that girl
the girl I saw in a crowd once saw in a crowd once. See?

It's only a matter of time before she sleeps with me.

ITMA

Honeymooning couples blithely hanging out
the DO NOT DISTURB or a Cockney shout

of 'Taxi!' Stewed prunes. All worth a giggle
to them then. The belly dancer's wiggle

of plenty, tawny flesh in a sheik's harem.
A gust up a lady's skirt? They'd scream.

The Great War past, that man about to come:
I suppose we must forgive them.

Poor Noel Coward, sainted for his tat:
today we'd hang him high (if that

were not pernicious). Bones through noses,
and flower fairies teasing in the roses,

next to nothing on, a sort of kiddie porn
for aesthetes. The past is thick with corn

we wouldn't touch, we who have premature
nostalgia, a predilection for the pure

emphatics of the recent: a Seventies rich
with pre-modern, post-evolution kitsch

and spells with fever. Easy to get smitten.
The past rolls over, begs to be rewritten.

Stay calm. We've seen the future and its name
is more or less more of the same.

See, there's Strummer kicking in his amp
and, outside, Formby leaning on a lamp.

Show and Tell

Astrid brought an oxhorn
on which a sailor uncle carved her name;

Glen, a singing cricket in a jar.
By and by, the class were introduced

to copper sulphate crystals in a tube,
an urchin shell that still smelt of the sea.

When at last they came to me, my heart
beat like a vulture chick in a wren's egg.

All night long, Jesus had been whispering
the sweet words in my ear, until I knew,

but now I stood, my hands cupped empty,
pearl tears on the red puff of my cheeks;

their laughter booming down the blue hall,
shaking the little coats on their pegs.

The Beginning of the End

When my ex-wife found magnetic north
in my sock drawer,
I forecast the beginning of the end.

She invited over the neighbour who found
the centre of gravity
thumbed below the surface in the sugarbowl.

They phoned the police who very soon
were squeezing a slew
of anti-chaos from a Fairy Liquid bottle.

The sniffer dogs weren't far behind them
and made a beeline for
the rug below which lay Grand Unified Theory.

Soon there were swarms of officials
tugging at the missing link,
fingering the blade-sharp end of my Möbius strip.

I knew I'd have their deaths on my conscience
when they opened up
the drying cupboard and found inside

the nine-tenths of the iceberg which usually
lies below the water
which I'd been saving for a rainy day.

Gillian Ferguson

SCOTLAND ON SUNDAY

Selection from: *Air for Sleeping Fish* (1997) and *Baby* (2000).

GILLIAN FERGUSON's poems draw upon her intense but dislocated contact with the natural world to interpret many subjects, from love and motherhood to illness and death. Although a city-dweller and journalist, her imagination is rooted in the country, using a painter's palette of vivid, unexpected colours and her own personal yet unsentimental symbolism of flowers. 'Her poems are beyond mere nature description; gorgeous illuminations of private moments of love and fear' (Kathleen Jamie). 'Imaginative, brave, daring, and sometimes opulent, she is a marvellous addition to the number of younger Scottish writers' (Douglas Dunn). ●

Gillian Ferguson writes:

Last century there was a language of flowers, understood by lovers and friends. Messages of love, regret, hope, could be sent, and the symbolic qualities of flowers are seen even in ancient Egypt's blue water-lilies for a full harvest, and the Renaissance's white lily, emblem of purity. It was not until somebody else pointed it out, however, that I realised how far I had unconsciously developed my own personal flower symbolism, weighing down all manner of unsuspecting flowers, grand and small, with my own meaning, my own emotion.

Again and again flowers turn up during love, hate, illness, joy, fear and peace. As they make themselves seemingly out of nothing, from dry seed, they have an energy which I want to tap into; somehow flowers are able to connect earth, sky, and water, and they have that gently explosive, irresistible quality of nature as they burst slowly into bloom, into colour. A strange language for a townie, perhaps, to develop, but when I became pregnant and then had a new baby in the spring, this sense of connectedness to the energy of flowers allied to riotous hormones saw me continually dashing down to the nearby Botanic Gardens and having to restrain myself from not just touching all the flowers but shoving them in my mouth! Not something the police in charge of the immaculate Gardens would have appreciated. Even the baby does not escape: in one poem his fluffy aureole of blond hair is a dandelion clock, while in another an unfurling daffodil believes the baby related to itself due to his flower-like freshness. But baby, knowing nothing yet of his mother's language of flowers, ate the daffodil in question!

Winter Sunflowers

You cradle mouthless smiling flowers
through sparkled streets, bending winds,
yellow heads heavy in your crooked arm –
haloes in the grope of twilight.

Earth fish, summer snow, winter sunflowers –
an impossible gift races your heart home;
a torch to France's burning fields,
armies of flowers in rooted rows –

tournesols craning laden green sinews,
straining sky and eye to be more blue.
The sure colour of a child's sun
has sparked your January eyes,

a spring in their leaf shades
that thirsty summer crisped;
the seeds of grinning health.
Bold black single eyes

are laughing in their fat-petalled skirts
at thin lilies in serious moon-white gowns –
we hold solar blooms like cheerleaders.
Staked by our own two skeletons

we stand watered in the winter
eclipse of the dark days fallen –
born in the blind earth of life
love grows us like light.

Fear of the Future

Around flowers,
the sun draws coloured haloes;
sainted, green-haired earth –
a minefield in pastoral disguise.

Yawning air does not fool me —
explosions lurk,
will rip its throat
like hounds on deer and fox.

I bruise petals
with my heavy sole,
smell their blood —
I even fear butterflies

might fall and shatter
like kaleidoscopes.
My breath is tiny pieces of wind —
I know the rabbit's paralysis.

The Winter Rose
(for Dr James Hawkins)

Blue-handed, with difficult string,
I staked the broken winter rose,

unbending fibres of green spine,
lifting a crumpled white face —

rain-teared, blinded with earth;
finished by axing winds.

So many thorns hid in the leaves,
and light so thin,

my task lasted even as snow
rehearsed Christmas in the garden.

And when I would have drowned
in snow, an angel came —
I had no words or gold.

But I saw the crushed bush
ghosted with buds;

her face now upturned — furred,
snug in snow — to stars;

after sleeping summer
ironing new petals with air.

And when I would have drowned
in snow, an angel came –
I had no words or gold.

Silent as Roses

When there is too much to say
then we are silent –
silent as roses

whose red hearts
shout love
above the blood-drawing thorn.

Our stiff lips a dam,
tongues drown,
wet lashes excruciate.

As sea speaks to crushed shells,
sun to clouds it burns,
moon to dying stars,

we fill
day and night
with our silence.

Scan

In me a moonscape of organs,
bloodless, maybe a monster;

my blood thuds. Until a black
bubble. Silent, slow as a flower,

opening from limb buds,
an anemone pulse of fingers.

Under my thick skin veil,
not me, plugged; blind,

bulb-headed, spinning invisible
tissue on bones fine as fish.

Mouse-big, sparrow-hearted,
it becoming you, new from

nothing; the miraculous alien,
eel-supple in blank dreams.

And like men loving the blue
planet, the world is changed.

Inhaling His Hair

I inhale my baby's
dandelion hair –

failed fingers, cheeks,
envy nose and air

feeling white filaments
finer than the burn

of snow on skin,
clumsy dust crashing

swans' rough wings.
An aroma of clouds,

sun scent, in this summer
aureole, seeded scalp.

Jane Holland

Selection from: *The Brief History of a Disreputable Woman* (1997).

JANE HOLLAND is a former women's snooker champion, banned for allegedly 'bringing the game into disrepute', an experience she draws upon in her poetry and in her novel *Kissing the Pink*. 'She entered a man's world where the battle to overcome bigoted rules and attitudes was as great as the battle to perfect her own skills in the field. She has turned her formidable energies and skills to poetry now with similarly turbulent and successful results' (Maura Dooley). 'A shrewd, sensitive, pained and perceptive outsider...she uses language both as a weapon and as a shield...an intelligent book, knife-sharp at moments, tender and gentle at others' (Brendan Kennelly). ●

Jane Holland writes:

I've only ever written two poems about snooker and 'Baize Queens' is mercifully the shorter of the two. I wanted to get across the brashness and caustic humour of women players: ambitious, defiant, surviving and *succeeding* in spite of the odds stacked against them.

I'm continually fascinated by how poetry works, what it consists of, and 'Wavelength' is an attempt to look at form: in particular, effects produced by white space left by line and stanza breaks.

Stylistically closer to the poems I'm writing now, 'Sleep' comes from a long poem called *Umbra* which I later rewrote as a verse play. I wrote these lines on a train, which started me thinking about the rhythms behind journeys, the way life can lull you to sleep with its sameness if you're not constantly watchful, ready to change direction at a moment's notice.

'Having read up on the subject' is an early poem which came directly from reading John Ashbery's *Self-Portrait in a Convex Mirror*. I was then also reading British poets influenced by the New York School – a dynamic combination which encouraged me to loosen my own approach to poetry. Essentially about memory, and how it acts before, during, and after the writing process, I also wanted to communicate that bizarre sense of arbitrariness involved in writing a poem. What inspires is not always something poetically-charged. Simply having dinner or getting dirt in your eye is more likely to provoke poetry than a great view or a crucial life event, probably because you're not blocking the "reception" by looking too hard for connections.

Baize Queens

We know this is not life.
Life does not have these corners
cut to pockets on the baize.

We take it oh so seriously though.
We fight to put the black away.
This is not life

but it's as near as dammit
when the green's running smooth
as silk and you're thirty points ahead.

This is not big money, no.
Not for women anyhow,
but still we do it all for love

or so they like to tell us.
This is our battleground.
Like Amazons,

we'd cut our tits off just to win.
We bitch in bathrooms
at the interval

and have our fill
of men who pat our heads
and pat our bums

and show us how to screw
or hold the cue
and ram it up their arses

if we're lucky.
Still, it's just a game.
Always shake her hand

and never cheat. Well played.
That last black really wiped its feet.
Give me a broom

I'll clear the bloody table.
This may not be life
but it's as near as dammit, girls.

Wavelength

I build the perfect silence with my hands:
a pyramid of sorts, an arch, the gaping
mouth of Agamemnon's beehive tomb.

When all is said and done, what will remain
but silence? I've lost the will to speak,
but send my empty hands to seek new land.

They will come back. Will they come back?
Distilling words until no words are left
becomes a concentration of the mind,

an endless search for essences of sound:
the slack white sands, the echo of the hills:
will they come back? They will come back.

You'll know the perfect silence when it comes.
It has the outward look of architecture
(structured stress), the inward hum of bees.

It stands alone, discarding time as one
who, trusting, shrugs a raincoat to the ground
before the storm is through. No reckless jump

from words to space, but something planned,
a leap of faith, inevitable to those
who welcome it into their silent band.

Sleep

The green arch of the bridge says *sleep*
The low slope of the field says *sleep*
The vole, lowering its head in the hedgerow, says *sleep*

The evening smoke says *sleep*
The white wall and the white fence say *sleep*
The canal, turning and wending, says *sleep*

The grim army of pylons says *sleep*
The dream of the cows, dreaming, says *sleep*
The leaf, midway between green and gold, says *sleep*

The flat shock of the horizon says *sleep*
The red tiles of the station say *sleep*
The fierce heart, unbending, says *sleep*

and *sleep* again.

But the coiled snake of the soul, hissing,
retreating, slipping its leash
and beating its tail at the door of the heart
says *wake, wake* and *the fall is forever.*

Having read up on the subject

this is a straight-forward choice between
understanding and misunderstanding.
Not just for me, watching the thin line of the road
snake off into the distance under a sky
that could have been purple a minute ago

but is reaching a dull red as it sinks into shadow,
but for these also, letting the thin line of the print
take off into the distance under a sky
that has expunged every last drop of light now
like a wiped-down blackboard

at the end of a curiously long classroom.
But what does it matter how much it weighs
unless this is a barter-system, so that
each word like each tall strand of wheat
is exchanged for lunch under a hot sun, a grape-hung

patio poised high above a breath-taking view
at Les Baux de Provence for example
where the wind spits dirt in your eye
unless you shelter in the narrow doorways
or dart sideways down those long cool passages

to sun-struck terracotta, a veranda wasped
with honeysuckle, where *petites baguettes*
pile up in baskets by the door.
This then is where it ultimately leads:
not to some classic moment of inspiration –

ahhh! the light-bulb caught above your head –
but here, now, drinking wine with some friends
or dining alone above the white rocks at Les Baux,
knowing that soon it will be time for the long drive home,
the giving and receiving of keys,

the letters piled up in the porch, even the click
of the ansaphone signalling nothing
so that this minute, this hour, is somehow special:
worth remembering, taking apart later
like an airfix model, only to put it back

into its composite parts, or like bones, broken
but meticulously reset as they are rested.
There will come a time when even this is finished:
when there are no more bones to set
and that afternoon on the veranda

is nothing but a memory, a word
that someone read somewhere,
caught up, nodding but disorientated,
as one who having stumbled on a secret place
discovers they were not the first to have found it.

Jackie Hardy

Selection from: *Canuting the Waves* (1998).

JACKIE HARDY's voice ranges from gentle chiding and wry comment to bristling annoyance and edginess. In two of her particular specialities, parodies and haiku, the soul of her wit is levity as well as brevity. In *Canuting the Waves*, she challenges the unruly elements: while the Canute approach will not hold back the sea, it's human nature to give it a try. Other poems about relationships, gender and ageing muddy the not-so-calm waters of comfortable assumptions. 'Hardy's forays into family life are as unsentimental as her escape routes are unexpected...The sea is never far away, echoing her range – from a whisper to a roar' (Linda France). ●

Jackie Hardy writes:

In *Canuting the Waves*, I explore issues concerned with ageing, gender and family life, and this sometimes leads to unexpected insights, revelations and discoveries. My poetry also investigates the impetus behind control and surrender. I am interested in the way people operate along the continuum of abandon and constraint, something I'm aware of particularly in relation to myself. In the sonnet 'Wet Feet' I act as my own best friend and give myself some good advice, but as usual, I'm too headstrong to listen.

In 'The Difference', I'm both of the two women in the poem and I examine the problem that results when two of the many roles I play lead to contradictory desires. However much I want to be whole, ultimately, there is no reconciliation.

'Objection Overruled' was written after the publicity received by a rape case being heard by an out-of-touch judge. I had been angered by both the woman's subjection to further trauma in court and the subsequent media coverage. The form, rhythm and the effect of the repetition were borrowed from Simon Armitage's poem about Strangeways prison.

When I began an MA in Women's Studies in 1993, the most challenging thing I needed to do was to become computer literate. Simultaneously I began to reconsider the Genesis story. I pondered on how different women's lives might have been if our culture had absorbed the first creation myth, or woman had been created first, and these trains of thought resulted in 'Computer Aided Design: Creation'.

Wet Feet

What do you expect if you are always
King Canuting the waves? You're bound to end
up damp. Why can't you walk foot-stepped bays,
keep in the shadow of cliffs? As a friend
I offer this advice for what it's worth:
build your castles where others have built theirs,
avoid quicksands, give rock-pools a wide berth,
marsh and mudflats may catch you unawares.
Remember, be alert for wind-blown spray.
Walking that lacy line is never safe:
a little sand in your shoes will not weigh
you down, soon you will hardly feel it chafe.
It's no good thinking that your toes are webbed.
Come back! At least wait till the tide has ebbed.

The Difference

I left by the front door
and took the path
less gravelled. By
the love-lies-bleeding
I saw your face
in the window
and for once
we saw eye to eye.
At the weeping willow
I felt the warm yellow
of a smile on my back.

Later I crept
through the back door
to pick up the pieces;
the rest of myself.
There in the kitchen
you were cooking steak, naked.
Nipples hardened by fat spits,

legs freshly shaven,
you seemed to be
rubbing along
the right way.

I asked you
what you thought
you were doing
and could we
get together sometime?
You said
you thought I had split.
And that's how you wanted it.
Your smile
oranged to red
so I split again.

Objection Overruled

Not only the rape
but the tone of the questions.
Not only the rape
but the latent suggestions.

Not only the rape
but the media's mileage.
Not only the rape
the psychological damage.

Not only the rape
but the hints of temptation.
Not only the rape
but the judge's summation.

Not only the rape
but the lack of repentence.
Not only the rape
but the length of the sentence.

Not only the rape.

Computer Aided Design: Creation

In the beginning was the number cruncher.
On the face of it darkness screened.
God had cold feet, terminal–user worry.
He searched the void, put in a warm boot.
God logged on, remembered the colon
and there was light.

Then came the word. And the word was God
was trying to jump before He could run.
Hands on, God pressed space, split-screened heaven
and earth from the waters. At the interface
God inserted disks, backed up the system
with a graphic display.

The package had chips with everything,
so God got bold, accessed the menu in colour;
blocked the earth with green, the seas blue;
entered fish and fowl. With another byte
God updated fields, returned beasts, cattle
and creeping things.

He opened a window, watched them browse.
God saved beasts and cattle, scanned creeping things.
Somehow there were bugs in the system.
God reprocessed data, executed, maximised;
gave creeping things another pair of legs,
a sting in the tail.

Then God created first generation humans
in His own icon. To the female He gave
the second generation function, the womb,
so that she might be fruitful and multiply
even unto the millionth generation.
And He called her Wombman.

Then God copied the female, cut and pasted,
deleted the womb. And the male He called Man.
God scrolled through His works, monitored progress.
God saw that it was good and that His name
was in the hi-scores. Level six ended the session.
God logged off.

Clare Pollard

JOYCE POLLARD

Selection from: *The Heavy-Petting Zoo* (1998).

CLARE POLLARD wrote most of the poems in her *Heavy-Petting Zoo* while still at school in Bolton. She is now 20, much too young, perhaps, to expect anyone to take her seriously, but young enough to question that assumption and much else besides. Her poems are fresh and energetic, barbed with a modern girl's natural cynicism, but tempered with open-eyed hope as well as wry acceptance.

'This is work you can't ignore – raw, reckless and more bloody-minded than an older, so-called wiser poet would dare to be. Clare Pollard tells us what it's like to be young, slim and pissed at the dawn of the 21st century' (Selima Hill). ●

Clare Pollard writes:

The most important thing about my poems is the emotion. Three years' distance from them makes some lines seem clumsy and raw, but I hope they still have an intensity. 'The Heavy-Petting Zoo' is a favourite. I have a mania for extended metaphor and innuendo, and here I hit on the perfect vehicle for these. I think the imagery captures that cocktail of naïvety and bestiality that best sums up early sexual encounters.

'Breakfast Poem' was based on an embarrassing true-life incident. Sifting through last night's memories with a hangover is one of the most humbling experiences, and I don't think there are enough decent hangover poems. Using rhyme is unusual for me, but I hope it gives that sense of mindless repetition which you feel as you go through the motions of breakfasting with a hangover.

'A Friday Night at the End of a Millennium' is set in a dingy night club to which I was mysteriously drawn every Thursday and Friday night of my teenage years in Bolton. It was written mainly for the amusement of my friends, but does deal with ideas about waste of potential that occur throughout my work. Like many of my poems it has a strong narrative element, which I'm interested in as a way of getting people emotionally involved in my work.

Depression, longing and humiliation are fairly universal experiences, so I hope you don't have to be under eighteen to enjoy these poems, and that by writing as someone experiencing them for the first time I have given them a freshness that touches a few nerves.

The Heavy-Petting Zoo

It's your best friend's 16th birthday party.
That's eight hamster lives, and yet she still wasn't wise enough
to realise it would turn into a heavy-petting zoo.
Let's put it this way – you wouldn't bring the family,
and there's an awful lot of stroking going on.

The lounge crawls with muzzy, fuzzy pubic mice.
You want to hibernate, but every bedroom is locked.
(That soft-haired girl from the Shetlands is offering rides.)

You could have been a part of it –
for a small price at the door you could have had them
eating out of your hand by now,
felt that breathy, hot nuzzle-lick,
but instead you're floundering in your own sour
vinegar juices, like a sick terrapin.

The other girls are beautiful and brittle chicks,
eggs precarious and smashable in the cups of their bras,
and he's with her somewhere.

They're probably mewling cutely at each other,
or else she's stripped and pink as a piglet
and they're at it like rabbits.
It's sickeningly bestial.
You hope they get myxomatosis.

Yet in your small child's heart you know
that if he'd called you, you'd have followed him as she did.

As a lamb does, whitely and without question.

Breakfast Poem

I am egg-shell fragile and grapefruit sour.
My face blotchy; eyes raisins soaked in booze.
I stench of night-sweat, am too tired to shower,

to scrub off each ingrained mascara bruise.
Memories slice up my still-sleeping head,
the morning paper does not bring good news.

I'm strawberry-jam sickly; I'm bacon dead.
It's always morning when the ghosts appear –
they haunt my toaster and they burn my bread,

they say I stink as stale as last night's beer.
They laugh with glee to know I burned inside,
once aware that your skin was tasting-near.

I had no resistance; I had no pride.
Confessed my love, then watched you turn to run.
Now my egg tastes salt from tears I've cried,

my soldiers are charred black. No war is won.
I try to weigh my loss against my gain:
I have lost uncertainty, face and sun-

rise. I've gained a hangover; a dull pain.
We're out of milk. My party dress is stained.

from A Friday Night at the End of a Millennium

On the first of January
in the year 2000
I will be twenty-one.
Yes, I am a woman

of the next millennium;
star on the clean black.
Our hope for the future.
but I don't give a fuck

as I check my pocket:
purse, lipstick, rape alarm;
and I'm out for the night in a town
where only rain glitters.

Air slits up my wrists
as I head for the pub.
Tottering on thin heels,
a cripple.

* * * *

I enjoy dancing.
There is a kind of freedom in it,
energy pounding out
of my hunched-up joints.

From the floor I watch
a boy who told me he thinks
I am very attractive –
but he's sleeping with her now.

The big commitment –
get them in bed
and they're caged. Hooked.
Can't wriggle free.

His hair is chilli-red,
his eyes fish scales,
his smile a small boy's.
I used to get giddy when I saw him –

Now I just feel weighted.
Tired. My bones will shatter
like peanut brittle or barley sugar
or some other crap sweet.

Another pint, and they charge
me two pounds this time –
they must have seen me staggering,
but I'm too drunk to care.

Alcohol goes straight through me.
The girls' loos are full
of lads smoking joints,
so I have to piss quietly,

hovering over the bowl
as though I'm a hummingbird
in order to avoid diseases.
Stale urine.

Someone's bloody tampon goads me redly.
I read the sign on the toilet door,
it says: 'AVOID UNWANTED
PREGNANCY — USE A TELEPHONE.'

Oh, that used to make us laugh
when this bitter-dark club seemed new;
when this tongue-moist air
didn't catch in my throat

like a wishbone. I always wish
for something utterly impossible:
lager that hasn't been watered down,
a star, him.

The poor wish fairies —
I am expecting miracles!
It isn't fair on them.
This bad luck is my own responsibility.

It is my own fault,
I take all the blame.
I vow to aim lower and stop thinking
I'm the fucking second coming,

then pull up my silk copping-knickers.
Stumble out, eyes greyed
by a gauze of yeast.
Mirror, mirror on the wall,

says I'm the biggest dog of all.
My flaws glow vivid.
nuclear white light strips my skin off
and leaves the true-me clean.

Frieda Hughes

Selection from: *Wooroloo* (1999).

FRIEDA HUGHES's poetry extends the distinctive imaginative territory of her paintings and children's books. Her fables cast light on two worlds, giving a mythic dimension to contemporary life at the same time as they depict with an artist's keen eye the particular nature of beast, fish and fowl. Strange creatures and fabled beings come to life in her poems, so that birds and birdmen, fathers and family, the dying and the dead, swarm through the psyche like flames in a burning forest. Though a writer of unusual pedigree, she is first and foremost an original voice, with her own compelling stories to tell. ●

John Kinsella writes:

Frieda Hughes has a keen eye for people, relationships, animals, and life-force. She paints landscapes and portraits, and visualisations of the psyche. Death is here, but only because of the living.

Hughes's poems are largely formed by the tensions between the Edenic potential and potentially hellish reality of exile and isolation. Her book is about aloneness, about cathartic confrontation and rebirth. For Hughes, the world is alive. Even death is alive. She recognises its finality in fleshly terms, but examines the way it is animated through the interweaving of life and "nature".

We can have many lives, all interconnected. The human soul and human disquietude and hellishness inhabit all, but Hughes's poems restructure an often alien world to gain kinship with it, to open lines of communication in moments of the greatest despair. A poem such as 'Laszlo' shows how interaction with other people can be healing.

The presence of birds epitomises this: they symbolise the interconnectness of things. The small space can be the most infinitely complex, all nature is read and reads through them (as at the end of 'Bird'). As a Western Australian, from the same physical setting of poems such as 'The Different Voice', I feel a kinship with the tainted expositions of this rich and varied but flawed paradise.

She sees outside the self. The position of the confessional voice in this poetry is quite deceptive – the 'I' can be both public and personal. Such poems outflank the obvious. This is poetry come out of siege.

Bird

Flip-top with brain
At the beak back.
Mouth so wide open
Houses would disappear.
Continents cringe, curl their toes
And hang on to their oceans.

Maw with a jaw as wide
As whatever enters. Small mice,
Large cats, or middle-size rats
With twisted whiskers.
Its call hallows the black
That brings silence.

And the body bears feathers
In its quiet. Its little soul sleeps,
So small in its twigs.
If it yawns, or belches,
There is a city in there,
With its lights on.

Foxes

Christmas night. The three of us,
Eating steak and salad without
A relative between us, beside us,
Or even at the end of a table
That would sit twelve, if we had chairs.

He appeared at the floor-deep window,
A sudden little red thought. Lost,
When we looked, like a name on a tongue-end,
Never certain. Ear tips like a claw hammer,
Face like a chisel, then gone.

He was back, two bits later, whippet body
Wanting steak fat. Half grown,
His small feet black as match heads,
His nose not able to let
The smell of meat alone.

His very presence begged us for a bite,
Hungry in the houselight. And there she was,
Just as motherless. His sister,
Coming for dinner,
Threading the field like a long needle.

In the Shadow of Fire

They are fast in their cars
For the children, or the milk
Or their mother.

The sky sickens, its breath is stained
With the endings of trees.

If it comes nowhere close, then
We are brave in the face of it.
We must not run.

The sun opens its orange mouth, aghast,
And puts its face out.

A silence falls as if the land
Listens,
For which parts are screaming.

Three houses and one man
Are dead already.

We hose down our tiles and our tin
And close our doors against
The smell of sacrifice.

Somewhere fire lives, breeds,
Walks forward.

The Different Voice

The fox chewed his thoughtful paw, gnawed
At his own toes and knew his differences.

When he opened his sharp mouth, long tongued
And lined with hard white spires, his voice rose

Like the howl of a ripped tree gasping for roots.
This was not a fox noise. The others listened.

Opened their mouths and out fell their words,
Dumb little shrunken heads, scattering like walnuts.

They were not in the same pain. Could not see the life
In dying things, enough to weep their passing.

They turned him over, heaved him sideways
With their curiousness, looking for flaws.

He was so like them in hair-coat and footprint,
But that voice, that voice made their own breath freeze

Like ice fog in the lung, hit by fear. That voice
Opened muddy holes in their burrow, where fear sat watching.

The same sound peeled back their eyelids,
Made them squint and sour.

But they did not think to let that light drive out their terror,
Instead, they blocked up those new corridors.

They rolled their friend into a corner, no longer a friend
But something against which to pull on their ignorance,

Like coats in the cold for each of those who spoke the same.
Spoke often, to ensure that constant recognition.

Ships' horns in sea mist, or sheep,
Lost and stupid in their search for children

All so alike, only their echoes could reach across the distance,
Until mouths found nipples and skeins were gathered in.

In the back, in the dark, the single fox
Glittered. They had missed his gold.

Kookaburra

So big in life, head like a chopping block
Beak like a carving knife,
His hysterical voice cracked branches, his laugh
Stripped bark from the wood-borers.

But in the twilight something got him,
So close to the house I should have heard.
He was left like a taunt, a dead bird
By an empty chicken run.

Now his dusk-stained feathers rock
In their dead grass cradle,
His bitten body is the flame
From which these moths escape.

That beak is buried in the sucked-out skull
Where eyes were lost in another mouth. His small crate,
Ant-eaten already, has ribs open like rafters
To welcome flies, and his wings rest like two open fans
      beside him.

Stripped of what made him
He is only a fraction of his noise.

Birds

The poet as a penguin
Sat in his snow-cold, nursing
The egg his wife had left him.

There it was, born of them both,
Like it or not. Rounded in words,
And cracking open its shell for a voice.

In the blizzard,
Beaten up from the arctic flats
Were the audience.

From the glass extensions
Of their eyes, they watched
The skuas rise on the updraft,

Every snap of their beaks
Like the tick of a knitting needle,
Hitching a stitch in the wait

For a rolling head.

Laszlo

There were roses, first,
In my little fog-box
Where the nurse floated
With her one carnation.

His face followed, led
By a nose worth having a face for,
And his lips kissed.
The pethadine dripping into my tube

Almost took him from me. Bag-like, my belly
Gaped up at him with its stitched mouth,
Struck dumb from crotch to navel, my two halves
Trying to escape each other.

Intent, he listened to my breathing.
Then, light as dust, his hand
Rested on the row of bloody sutures
As if to make me whole.

Nick Drake

SIMON ANNAND

Selection from: *The Man in the White Suit* (1999) .

NICK DRAKE's poems portray and celebrate a richly varied cast of characters whose secrets and histories are the central thread of his book *The Man in the White Suit*. They range from life studies of those caught out by exile from central and eastern Europe or caught up in the strange aftermath of the 1989 revolutions, to intimate love poems and elegies, including several dedicated to friends who have died of AIDS.

'Nick Drake's début collection is subtle, funny and tremendously moving. He has an eye for the small detail as well as for the big picture. These poems brilliantly evoke time and place' (Jackie Kay). ●

Nick Drake writes:

There have been many men in white suits: Elvis in his late Las Vegas period, Martin Bell broadcasting from the war zones, Liberace in sequins on the cover of his *Greatest Hits*...but above all, Alec Guinness starring opposite Joan Greenwood in the 1951 Ealing comedy about a self-deprecating genius who invents a fabric which never gets dirty and never wears out; in the end the fabric has a fatal flaw and the immaculate white suit just dissolves.

The theme of the title-poem grew from a small moment; I was eating dinner with a brilliant Romanian friend in a dismal international restaurant in Bucharest; someone was singing 'Take My Breath Away', so slowly it ran backwards. I had been admiring the falling snow, but she contradicted me: '*That is not snow.*' I was baffled: '*It is, it's snow.*' '*No. That is SLUSH.*' She didn't mean just the snow; and she went on to deconstruct me, and my cocktail lounge romanticism, more or less as recounted in the poem.

'The Foley Artist' spends his working life in tiny rooms and gets an equally tiny credit at the end of the movie; but without him the film's sound-world would lack reality. He adds in all the aural detail of the characters' existence using a baffling gamelan of combs, sandpaper and gravel trays. (I think my Foley artist has been too long in his tiny room...)

'The Very Rich Hours' was written in memory of my friend Dave Royle, just one of a generation of gay men killed by a virus that has given cruel new life to the old association of beauty and mortality.

NICK DRAKE

The Man in the White Suit

Only the light industry of snow
was working in the derelict, curfew city;
a mid-winter night-shift, a hushed revelation
of ice-flowers or flakes of contamination.

We talked about angels: how you needed one
to guard you through these difficult dark days;
you watched as I fell back into a drift
between two cars and waved my arms for wings.

You did not smile. I only made it worse;
as we entered the Hotel Europa's concrete tower
through the revolving door's glass atmospheres,
and the blast of hot air melted everything

I joked I was the man in the white suit
playing cocktail lounge piano, arpeggios,
diminished sevenths, dedicated schmaltz,
serenading you, my Salome;

under the glitter-ball's decadent stars
you'd dance between the tables of businessmen
and currency girls whose shrugged-off furs
hung savage from their chairs; and we'd duet,

the accidental twins of East and West,
crooning each others' secret lives and loves,
the one true poem – but the dazzle stalled
when in perfectly bladed English you replied:

This is the new Europa of Yes or No,
of night-life, gambling and pornography,
luxury, uncertainty and despair;
of accusation and idealisation,

revenge and freedom and the gods'
bargains of the chances of a lifetime.
This is my prison; but you just play along
like Liberace, chronic and naïve.

And so how candidly you set my head
on its tarnished platter, my idiotic talk
stopped with a joke-apple garnishing
my gob-smacked jaw. Then you were going,

going, in the taxi's porphyry and rust;
you looked out at my snow and nailed it *slush*,
too wet to bear the image of anything;
and then the door slammed and you sped away

between the pot-holes, monuments and icy works
of your dark city, leaving me alone
in the revolving door, my fragile crown
and white suit melting on me where I stood.

The Foley Artist

*'A specialist in creating sounds, especially of body movement,
recorded to fit the pictures on the screen'*
THE COMPLETE FILM DICTIONARY

A strange calling; to play the minor effects,
the off-screen score you notice by its absence;
but in this small suitcase of tricks I hold
the bricabrac of people being there,
the world dismantled to its sticks and stones.
For instance; I can conjure my own approach
from foggy distances with a handful of pebbles;
the swish of corduroy, the creak of leather
are just two of several variations
played upon fine ribbons of sandpaper.
Paper torn is fire; an ounce of sand
hissing in a matchbox is the sea,
or the Sahara, or a deep sleep.
A mirage of ice is done with ice and glass.
Ten raindrops caught in zero gravity
can be a storm. A grain of salt is tears.
I could articulate the life and death
agonies of a snowflake, or this my grin.
With ebony, feathers, needles, smoke and dust
I have mastered all the little noises of war.

It is my music. Time is two tin hands,
one all-purpose twinkling tinsel star,
a splinter of moon-rock, and its tidal pull:
breath-mist fading on an inch of mirror.
Mystery is velvet, silver nitrate night.
Imagine me, now, alone in my dark room,
no words, no music, and no audience;
a hyperactive, lunatic one-man band
working to the speed of shadow and light,
tinkling, jingling, rattling, scratching, banging
from small Genesis to minor Apocalypse;
but I do the last frames like a dream:
a question mark, a balloon twisted awry;
a football rattle cranked; stopped with a nail;
and last the great arcana of smoke-rings
to create the loop-hole through which I disappear
as if I was never here.
And so this is the end; and please remember:
a slamming door is always a slamming door.

The Very Rich Hours
(for Dave Royle, 1960-1996)

His window frames our pictured, distanced city:
people, traffic, countless other windows,
the very rich hours of the land of the living.

Inside the golden sun illuminates
four vases of flowers, a plastic water-jug,
dust motes in the vacancy, and Dave in a red chair.

I sit facing his level, absent gaze
the muscles of anger and pleasure have withered to;
he does not know me: I hardly know him.

Each morning he is cradled in a bath;
his cigarettes burn down to his finger-tips;
all I can do for him is tap the ash.

Pitched against the gym's weights and measures,
discovered in the fluencies of the showers,
his body seemed to me a worked perfection;

he used it for spare cash and for the stories;
up cranky Soho stairwells, in gas-fire rooms
he modelled for "amateur photographers"

who tested him up close with their light meters,
and composed him – athletic, classical –
held still, 'Poetry!', for their camera fire.

Between a bureau de change and a cigarette kiosk
he'd return to London's arcane A-Z
of night life, bars, punters, strangers and friends;

there were dark back-rooms and moonless midnight parks,
shadows in the margins, the casual glory of skin;
desire, not the sorrow of desire.

Now mortality has become familiar;
his friends are dying, or gathered here, or both,
in this book of hours and hours of smoking and waiting

to turn the page; and nothing to be done
except to stay, so simple and difficult. Leaving,
I picture him for the last time, for myself;

his window discloses a dark, deserted city;
the traffic lights are changing on their own;
the moon repeats itself in countless windows.

The silenced TV casts its blue and silver,
the world's text, irrelevantly across
the parchment of his dream-skin;

the tattoed swallow soars from his right arm
and his slight weight; may tomorrow's sunlight
shine right through to illuminate his heart:

a Proper of Time, a brief history, a love story.

Amanda Dalton

CLAIRE McNAMEE

Selection from: *How to
Disappear* (1999).

AMANDA DALTON's poems shine a torch into
dark corners and find a world inhabited by
the missing and the dead, by monsters and
wounded beasts, discarded dreams and the
memories of strangers. 'Dalton's poetry is a
kind of ghost writing – as if she can revisit
herself, stand there among memories, real
and imagined, and be haunted by her own
presence' (Simon Armitage). 'Dark, funny,
wise, terrifying...She is searingly matter-of-
fact about the most painful recesses of the
human heart...This may be Dalton's first
book but she dances round every corner with
a grace that many more seasoned writers
would die for' (Jo Shapcott). ●

Amanda Dalton writes:

I had to call my book *How to Disappear* – so many of the poems
are inhabited by would-be disappearers and by those who try to
hang onto them, usually after they've gone. This "conjuring" doesn't
always entirely work: 'The Dad-Baby', for example, isn't a reassur-
ing father. But still, it's the *imaginative* life that keeps the dead, the
vanished and those who miss them, alive. And it allows for some
magical events and transformations.

Room of Leaves is a narrative sequence of seventeen poems. It
begins in 1959 when Grace, at last, falls in love, only to be jilted at
the altar. She sets up home in her mother's garden and waits, for
thirty years, for Frank to return. In part the sequence, in fact the
whole book, is about obsession: the near psychosis of certain kinds of
love; getting stuck with an idea or feeling; our fundamental need to
believe, and how that belief can endure, sometimes against all odds.

There's a child's vision, I think, in several of the poems. I like
the unembarrassed inventiveness of young children, their ability to
create strange and often very funny worlds and narratives at the
drop of a hat, and their open, direct way of stating what's what.

I'm interested in what happens when a matter-of-fact or "simple"
frame is used to explore highly charged or complex emotions. 'How
to Disappear', for example, offers a childish rite or set of instruc-
tions for the most desperate of adults; 'Kitchen Beast' places a
"wild thing" in the cupboard, like something from a picture book
– except it's grown-ups who discover it, whose relationship is pulled
apart by its presence.

The Dad-Baby

After your death, the fortune teller
told me to expect you
so I took to sitting in the dark
doing a kind of meditation.

Sometimes I thought I nearly saw you
gathering shape by the mantelpiece
and once I almost heard your voice
at the back of my neck –

but I was trying too hard,
so instead I watched TV
and started leaving all the lights on,
and sure enough that was when you came.

The trouble was you came as the Dad-Baby,
all hunched and cramped
in a pram that was never ours.
Only your grey eyes were familiar

and your gold tooth
grotesque in an infant's face.
Old balloon-head bobbing up
and back behind the blue canvas hood;
then you were gone.

Kitchen Beast

It was a mild spring.
No wonder he left the kitchen door ajar,
no wonder the grey-eyed beast came in
and squeezed into the cupboard
underneath the sink.

It was a still and weathered thing
you might mistake for stone, except
in very quiet times, she heard its rasping breath
and, if she sniffed the air,
she thought she could detect a whiff of zoo.

She blamed him, for leaving doors wide open.
He blamed her for showing him
the beast that he'd let in.

It was a case of fear, she knew.
The bulging kitbag packed in minutes,
tow rope, book of knots he grabbed
as he ran for the hills
without a single *sorry* or *goodbye*.

It was a mild night.
She left the kitchen door ajar
and set about creating quite a careful trail
of milky drinks and cabbage leaves and ham,
in little bowls across the floor, for coaxing.

How to Disappear

First rehearse the easy things.
Lose your words in a high wind,
walk in the dark on an unlit road,
observe how other people mislay keys,
their diaries, new umbrellas.
See what it takes to go unnoticed
in a crowded room. Tell lies:
I love you. I'll be back in half an hour.
I'm fine.

Then childish things.
Stand very still behind a tree,
become a cowboy, say you've died,
climb into wardrobes, breathe on a mirror
until there's no one there, and practise magic,
tricks with smoke and fire –
a flick of the wrist and the victim's lost
his watch, his wife, his ten pound note. Perfect it.
Hold your breath a little longer every time.

The hardest things.
Eat less, much less, and take a vow of silence.
Learn the point of vanishing, the moment
embers turn to ash, the sun falls down,

the sudden white-out comes.
And when it comes again – it will –
just walk at it, walk into it, and walk,
until you know that you're no longer
anywhere.

from Room of Leaves

In Love

Look at me now, mother,
your awkward lump,
dancing with Frank to *Moonglow*
and knowing the words.

I've worn my American stockings to the 3D film
and I'm tipsy on gin.
would you believe it?
Please try

then next time you tell me I stare like a simpleton
perhaps I'll explain how I'm learning
to see Frank's face on the bedroom wall
whenever I choose.

We've been looking at rings, mother.
My favourite is blue.
Please serve a chicken on Sunday
and smile.

Nest

I'm building a nest in the garden
and watching my breath disappear
into splintered trees.
The sky is scratched and freezing;
birds are trapped in it.

I finger veins on damaged leaves
and put my ear to the cracked soil

but there's no pulse.
My nest will be of dead and aching things,
lined with my wedding dress,
decorated with our broken flowers.

I'll sing a marriage song behind my throat
where everything is cold and trapped.
Save me from losing my breath in the hard air.
Save me from screaming like birds
and wondering how things disappear.

I'm setting up home without you,
unpacking my trousseau in a room of leaves,
singing.

Almost Bird

Watch.
I can balance like this for hours,
branched high, with my marble eyes
jabbing at weevils.
And I can crouch with my head cocked
to hear the worms underground.

I'm just waiting for wings now,
for that moment of lift
as the wind takes me.
I'm waiting to hang in the air.

Look, claws.
And here's a lichen
spreading down my broken veins.
Every joint in me is knotted.
Is that good?

I know that I can fill a field
with flapping and I can pitch
the harsh note for alarm.
But I am egg empty. I am cold.
There is a cave in me
and its voice reverberates
along my hollow bones.

Christiania Whitehead

Selection from: *The Garden of Slender Trust* (1999) .

CHRISTIANIA WHITEHEAD's poems inhabit a garden walled like a medieval retreat, a place of imaginative seclusion where she confronts the tensions between a living faith and a lived, sensual life. From this Eden set within the modern world, its foliage barely veiling the tensions of desire, she emerges from the fight with God with these jewel-like poems. Hers is a poetry as much filled with wonder and transcendence as with the pleasures and perils of flesh and friendship.

'The great strength of Whitehead's poems is their mixture of eroticism and mystery, their focus on that place where God meets sex' (Jo Shapcott). ●

Christiania Whitehead writes:

Rhythm and linguistic richness are primary concerns within my poetry. Not that I pursue any authorised beat. But there's still always a kind of underground music that I'm trying to be truthful to, and I'll often go back and rewrite a line several times just to arrive finally at a pattern of stresses which feels lyrical. Language, the same. I look for *meatiness* in words. Words which one can shake between the jaws and chew upon! I'm fascinated by the subliminal secondary meanings lying beneath words, and the way those meanings shift when you change to a new context. It's like placing a colour beside different contrasts – it alters completely.

And I also like a voice which is casual, even beguiling, before one realises the steel hunched beneath the velvet. 'Marian Hymn' and 'Brutus' Last Song' both speak with that sort of voice: they're lullabies designed to divert attention from the forthcoming stab in the back. 'Girls Sitting Together Like Dolls' has a slightly similar bite, although as a poem it's less mocking and detached, and more personally frightened. Judy's the one holding the dagger in this instance; Elly, the one who realises too late that cloaking the day in lullabies and child's games leads to disintegration.

My poems often sit upon thresholds of anticlimax or frustration. 'Morning Thesis' describes a dawn which breaks badly – a terrible dilution of purpose after great expectations; 'Daybreak' describes one which breaks well. Wonder isn't all that common to me, but when it comes I sense that it has more to do with nouns of spirited aggression – 'wire', 'strong white teeth of foam' – than anything soft.

Marian Hymn

Her goodness leaves scores on the skin
and all of that marital trousseau untouched.
Pictures in frames of herself that can
never come out, for she drags up the frames
to herself. No, she glances them there
with her toe. She hardly moves,
yet they come. Frames of the saint
and the virgin. Icons at least.
Devotional texts. Working the bloom
of the fame, of a babe without sex.
Curiously wan in the daylight.

Merely her hair is a signal to prayer,
or an invite for candles
to blacken and wreck. I want,
perforce, your mouth stopped from
this wonderland talk of umbrellas
and birds, this hiding in dells
of sly knowing silence;
this cotton! this wool! this
magnolia made to be kissed, bit
and left. I'll sue you at breakfast
for your freezing up eggs and then
chopping down men.

Girls Sitting Together Like Dolls

Judy likens the day with Elly,
to a cooking pot, to a steak full of juices, to
something their can lay their tongues on
and sweep along. And they
rustle their minds gleefully at this
secret metaphor.

Elly, making a pot of tea, calls it
a skull, that they may be drinking
from inside the pot. Judy loves
the idea of this good head syrup
they're getting down them.

The two girls create a crag of fruit
for every inch of their lovely skin.
Then they sit, realising everything is
not included. Elly slips
edibility into her perfect mind.

At the trial, when the judges asked where
was Elly, they found pips and stuff
in a trunk by the wall. They found Judy
at lunch on her quaint ways; on her
idiom of awkwardness, on her
artistic self.

Brutus' Last Song

Caesar's back, and they've built him a throne to sit on.
Get back to nature, Caesar. We've got you a tree stump;
broad as your kingly bottom. Magisterial.
Older than you'll ever be.
And when you rise from your wooden cradle,
black marks upon your robes'll tell
the people where you've been.

Ah, but when you sit now, that's really something.
See that bush, like a marvellous African head-dress
full of yellow whips, their tops dipped with blood;
or jugular red-hot pokers, who decided to take
a day off and wave a finger at your majesty.

Why, your majesty, see how, when you sit there,
they radiate around you.

One could almost believe you were going to die.

Morning Thesis

Sweetly breathed morning,
when you come over
the hill top as some steely

Lazarine monster, paring
oranges and oregano from
your fingernails, how often

you stop short on the summit
of the hill, hastily swallow
all the Pantheon smoke

you were preparing to exhale,
rearrange your metal facets
and cusps into reverse,

and scuttle away rearwards
executing a furtive sepulchral
courtship dance

back toward your
catacombs on the east
side of the world.

The Grass Crust

You've pulled back, like
a shadow blackening over

the grass crust
and savaging the clarity

of things. Without a hint,
a long hold, or a kind

of savoury twilight where
the rip might leave

threads like hyphens
of old blood

on either side. Instead,
a snap at midday,

a little astronomical thing,
sloughing off the heart

and all contentment
with its asteroids of will.

Daybreak

From the top of this bank I am able
to examine the first line of the day.
Not even a paragraph, only a few
black squiggles and semi-colons
of faith that read out of the sky
to the dawn, abandoning grammar.

The word *blue* comes scuttling along,
executes a half bow and awkwardly
disappears. It is a very early word.
It dwelt here, crept around
and had independent yearnings
when the earth was still a fistful
of slivers and impulses. It
knows it and is ashamed.

Your tongue dampens your lips,
words are no longer necessary.
Overhead, the gloaming seems to
withdraw. All your loveliness
is clenched in strong white teeth
of foam, the grass becomes
wire at your signal
and the morning breaks.

Polly Clark

DAVID BROWN

Selection from forthcoming
first collection (2000).

POLLY CLARK shows the complex and often
brutal making of a self in her poems, from
first passions, through losses and disappoint-
ments, to attempts to understand and for-
give origins. The forces which shape who we
are take on many personalities: surgeons,
horses, Amazon parrots and huge beetles
all have lessons to teach about loss, bereave-
ment and the shaping of a fragile identity.
Who decides who we are and what we will
be? Her journey encompasses diverse loca-
tions, from her native Canada to Edinburgh
Zoo, demonstrating that places can be as
important as people in shaping our internal
landscape. ●

Polly Clark writes:

My poems often relate to my life in a specific way: for instance the
poem 'Zoo' arises from a period when I worked as a zookeeper.
Like a lot of young girls (and I was 16 at the time), I fell heartily
in love with what I perceived to be "masculinity" and the physical
and exotic setting of a zoo served only to enhance my myth-making
tendency in that direction.

It was in this setting that I learned the first harsh lessons about
who I was, or at least who I was expected to be, and 'My Life with
Horses' takes this further. One of the things I'm trying to show in
this poem is the subtle change in my relationship with that power-
ful idea, and what becomes a race to its inevitable conclusion. It's
important though to stress that while these poems are in that most
obvious sense autobiographical, it is also the least important aspect
of them to me. My 'Excitement' is of course particular to me, but
the stuff of passion, its impact, its violence of feeling, its somewhere
undercurrent of unease is something I'd like to think I evoked, even
just a little bit, in you.

Similarly, in being an attempt to look squarely at a particular
death, 'Kleptomaniac' is also an evocation of one feeling in the
spectrum of emotions that accompany grief, as well as a picture of
a kind of relationship in life.

The hope that unites these poems is that I can *make you see what
I see.* And, even better, that you might go on from there to some-
where new, entirely your own.

Zoo

I remember kicking the bales down
from the top of the barn, my eyes streaming.

The only creature I truly loved
hugged me, and I thought his animal warmth

was more wonderful than the touch on my cheek
from the gibbon with the circular brown eyes.

The orang utan liked to scrub with a rag
and poke her leathery fingers through the bars,

and the elephant stood at the railings, curling
her trunk at the children,

her ears like rags, and her tusks
wrenched out; I thought

suffering must have a language, I loved
where love was wasted.

When the silly pop-eyed Père David
escaped across the zebras' frozen savannah

he chased it and threw
his great shoulders at its hooves,

bringing it down in a trembling
thump; and I thought the breaking

of freedom was beautiful, I thought
I was discovering truth

in these limbs collapsing,
antlers falling against the sky,

and the snow in shreds
like a man's blue eye.

My Life with Horses

Before I knew there were men
I galloped a pony bareback;
it was a hard winter, but
how sure-footed we were, resolute
in frozen emptiness, stamping
the ice with our names.

Years later I lay like a foal in the grass,
wanting to touch your hair;
we clutched like shadows,
I twined the past through my fingers, kissing
great gulps of father, of mother,
galloping, with nothing to stop me.

Now in the evening I put on my dress
like a secret; will you see
how my elbow pokes like a hock,
the way I have carefully cut my mane,
the way my eyes roll from fear of you?
I'm trying to hide the animal I am;

and you give me a necklace,
bright as a bit, and you're
stamping your name
into the earth, and my arm
is around you, weak as a halter,
and nothing can stop me, no mother or father.

Excitement

The day has blinked, the streets are awash with blue,
the mood of God is lonely;
all day he sent his frozen grief away, unfettered
it swirled and tumbled, unaware of falling.
All day I've waited on the inside,
watching the light grow fat and fade away.

God doesn't know of my excitement,
look my hands are neatly folded.
God doesn't know I've been possessed,
look I'm bright and smartly dressed.
But my heart's a lump of you,
I'm an empty bed at empty noon;
I'm a stone wall smacked with sunlight,
I'm a stick of rock with KISS stamped through.

Walk in the Rain

You walk for miles beside me
through trees that open out too quickly
onto rain-soaked common land.
I tell you almost everything,
I feel it coming out of me, like a sickness.
And you sit beside me
on a bench sodden with rain and the smell of things over
and you're telling me all those things are over,
and you're kissing me because they're all over,
and our bodies drift like leaves on the water,
and the people in the distance are made of water,
and the lake is swallowing, with a million mouths a second,
all the things I ever wanted, all the things that are over.

Kleptomaniac

There are things which you gave me:
a bundle of letters written in green,
a man's nose, a curly way of writing 'P';
and there are things which I *took*:
this unsmiling photograph,
this t-shirt, the taste of you washed out of it.

In a bright hospital
you offered your death to me.
You gave it slowly over months
then crazily, hand over fist.
You let me come when others must not come.
You let me sit beside you through the night.
This is vulnerability, the gift tag said,
your gift to me.

But of course it wasn't enough.
I couldn't stop a habit so long engrained.

On the last night, I snatched
a long look at you when we were alone.
I half-inched
a touch from your hand on my mouth
that you would never have allowed.
I lifted
your smile at the sound of my name
and I ran with it.

Like a stolen child
that all of Scotland Yard
and all the world's fathers are searching for,
I shut it in a dark place
where I wrapped it
over and over
in my delight.

Joanne Limburg

CHRIS HADLEY

Selection from *Femenismo*
(2000).

JOANNE LIMBURG wears comic camouflage to stalk serious subjects, from self-doubt and guilt to bereavement and its tangled aftermath. Her often boisterous poems celebrate the defiant vulnerability of modern women, exploring their lives as daughters, mothers, friends and rivals, as well as the never-ending struggle to keep body and soul on speaking terms, while under attack from within and without, whether by envy, depression, insomnia, oppression, mirrors, misogyny or just other people. They address the experience of being a Jew in the West at this point in history, with an awareness of the debt she owes to stubborn and resilient ancestors. ●

Joanne Limburg writes:

Nothing comes from nothing: I tend to think of my poems not so much as original creations but more as arrangements of words and images which I collect and then use to express my own preoccupations. When I write, I draw on English-language poetry but also on nursery rhymes, everyday speech, hymns remembered from school and the cadences of Jewish prayer.

'The Queen of Swords' was inspired by the image on a tarot card. It made me think about words we sometimes use to describe people which relate to knives: so-and-so is sharp-witted, says cutting things, and so on. There is a knife-edge, too, between surgery and assault, between helpful and bitchy.

'Seder Night with My Ancestors' takes its form from the Seder, which is the service held in the home on the first two nights of Passover, to celebrate the Exodus. At its centre is a question-and-answer session in which the younger members of the family ask their elders what on earth all this religious observance is for – and get a very firm response.

When I set out to write 'Barton in the Beans', I thought that it was going to be a sort of hymn of praise to English names and places, but it wound up as a burial. I think my sarky 'Inner Bloke' must have hijacked it.

'The Return' is about another form of possession, one of a group of poems I wrote after the death of my father. Strange things happen to a soul in mourning and I tried to use writing as a way of expressing and coming to terms with them.

The Queen of Swords

Every few weeks or so, I make
an appointment with this woman to tidy
my head up and trim my ends. It's risky.
On my way in, I often pass

some of her other clients holding
bloody rags to ears or necks —
she frequently forgets herself
in her eagerness to do you good.

But I'm not scared of the sharp gleam
in her eye when she tells me what
my problem is. It's the sign of the clearest
eyesight, a diamond of a mind.

Seder Night with My Ancestors

On this night,
my ancestors arrive,
uninvited but expected,
to have their usual word.

They sit around the table
but refuse my offer of food.

I switch the television off
and wait,
the air thickening
with disapproval.

At last I ask them:
What do you want from me?
What have you got to do with me?
Why do you come here, every year
on this night?

And what do they say?

They say:
For this God brought us forth from Egypt?
For this we starved in the desert?
For this we fled the inquisition?
For this we fled the pogroms?

Did we die
refusing unclean meat
for you to fill your fridge with filth?

Did we disguise
our Hebrew prayers
with Christian melodies
so that you could forget them?

For you we did these things?
Do you think the Lord
would have thought you worth saving?

I say that all I want
is to live my life.

Without us you would have no life.

Barton in the Beans

For comfort on bad nights,
open out a map of Middle England

and sing yourself to sleep
with a lullaby of English names:

Shouldham Thorpe, in gentle sunshine,
Swadlincote, in a Laura Ashley frock,

Little Cubley, veins running with weak tea,
Kibworth Beauchamp, praying on Protestant knees,

Ashby-de-la-Zouch saying 'Morning',
Wigston Parva, smiling – but not too widely,

Ramsey Mereside, raising an eyebrow,
Eye Kettleby, where they'd rather not talk about it,

Market Overton, echoing with the slamming doors
of Cold Overton, where teenagers flee every night to their rooms,

screaming that from Appleby Magna to Stubbers Green
they never met a soul who understood.

They never met a soul.
At Barton in the Beans, the rain says *Sssshhhhh...*

Inner Bloke

When I feel like a drag queen
in tights and heels,
I put that down
to my Inner Bloke.

He's the one
who always has to win,
who comes into his own
in seminars and pub debates.

He knows a lot of facts
and loves to swap them.
There's nothing he won't
turn into a joke,

including me.
He's a bully like that
and needs to put me down.
He's a thwarted thug

and it's all thanks to me,
the body he lives through,
my puny little arms,
that girly way I kick.

The Return

Dad,
I come home
and find you sitting
in every room in the house,
its smell your smell,
as if it were a jacket
you'd only just thrown off,
still warm.

As the house recalls you,
so do I,
resurrecting you
fifty times a day,
in the way you clench my teeth
when something fails to work,
as we prowl in step together
round my room,
hours into the night,
as you fret me into being ready
an hour early for every journey.
As I bite into something undercooked,
I feel you pull
that comical, disappointed face.

You prefer to hide
in better foods:
strong cheese, strong coffee,
anything sweet.
I find myself eating
a whole quarter of wine gums
just to give you
twenty more minutes
of borrowed life.

Jane Griffiths

MATTHEW POWER

Selection from forthcoming
first collection (2000).

JANE GRIFFITHS is a poet of place who belongs
nowhere. She lived in Holland from the age
of eight, and writes about the difficulty of
belonging in any one place or any one lan-
guage. Like many in the modern world, she
is estranged inside her own country, wherever
that is. In her intently observed poems, lan-
guage becomes her flesh and blood, while the
physical world is less than usually solid. Fields
are evanescent, and houses seem to be under
water. In the face of shifting boundaries, her
poems are attempted repossessions. The exile
comes home in the act of writing the poem,
finding it was always there, where she imag-
ined it, not where she thought it was. ●

Jane Griffiths writes:

I've always been surprised by the different ways in which experi-
ences can work themselves into writing. The first two poems here
draw on my childhood abroad, but whereas 'Emigrants' is an almost
literal record of my family's first afternoon in Holland, when my
father and I left my mother waiting for the furniture in an empty
house with concrete floors and no carpets, and went out to buy a
boat and one hundred curtain rings, 'Migration' approaches the
subject of exile more obliquely, concentrating on the emigrant's
habit of mind rather than her actual surroundings.

Curiously, although I'd always thought of it as a poem about
finding a poetic voice, I realise now that 'Lost and Found' is also
about bilinguality: a confused condition where no matter which
words you use, you're aware of the ghosts of other words underly-
ing them, and language becomes what MacNeice called 'incorrigi-
bly plural'. I no longer sound like a native Dutch speaker, but the
knowledge remains that meaning is rarely pure, and never simple.
When I use the word 'articulate', it has nothing to do with fluency,
but more with achieving a balance between all possible senses of a
word, allowing it its full, almost physical weight. It is this which I
explore in 'Errata'. Although its immediate inspiration was an actual
errata slip, and although the poem clearly draws on my work as a
letterpress printer in the late 1980s, its subject (as in 'Migration')
is the need to make a coherent story of dislocation and inconsis-
tencies, not only drawing on experience, but rewriting it, giving it
a recognisable form.

Migration

First, there was the waking,
each day, to a lightness
they couldn't place. The air
stretched tight as a sheet;
the sun on their whitewashed

walls was flexible, or at any rate
warm and rounded to the touch.
It clung about them; they moved
shadowless, footsteps dropping like
stones to the light-resounding bay.

Daily their home gathered weed,
names, string. Sea-changed,
their eyes lost transparency;
they saw the house as it was:
a wholly new thing.

When the dreams came:
tarred and feathered bundles
of prehistory, their webbed feet
clay. They came overnight,
silently, as homing birds

to their owners, whose waking
each day was to a clogged grey
dawn, whose night-time shadows
had wings, scything steeply
above their narrow beds.

Emigrants

Will know where they are by the absence
of trees, of people – the absence
even of anything to do. All
luggage is in transit; nothing at all
to do but watch from the empty house

through the empty window. The sky
is underlit, and under the sky
a lake, pewter, reflecting; a road.
Yellow buses turn at the end of the road,
if it is an end. Reeds block the view:

this bus is wheel-deep in them; it swims
along the lake's edge and a swan swims
towards it. They pass. And here, at last,
are two people, waiting for the last
bus out, or just standing, as people must

stand here often, leaning on the wind,
deep in reeds, and speechless in the wind
as if *lake* and *sky* were foreign words
to them as well: standing without words
but without need of them, being at home.

Lost and Found

On Wednesday last, in the vicinity
of the Kingston Road: item: one voice,
exact tenor and timbre unknown
but believed to be romantic (perhaps
something of a drifter). Frequently
sighted in the past by overnight travellers
on trains and coaches, in open-mouthed,
incessant, disembodied discourse
on the far side of the glass.
Believed to be making for the coast.
(Boat-owners please check your sheds.)

Its hideouts are various and it's rarely
in the same place twice but you'd know
it if you found it. It might be in the silence
when a crow stoops in a scything
graceline to pluck a leaf from the beak
of its own, moated reflection; it might be
floundering in the song sung by someone
rained on at a bus-stop, and although
you can't tell it by its gait or what it wears,
you will know it by the sense of suddenly,
incredibly, believing your own ears.

Errata

Page 1, line 8, for incorrigible read unredeemable
Page 5, line 9, for undeniable read indelible
Page 6, line 15, for unreliable read untellable

Dark, and the lights are out in all the houses.
The one streetlamp is swamped in sycamore,
all the hill's houses are cradled in root.
Leaves' shadow-selves crowd the walls like ivy.
The dark is laying it on thick, tonight.

Page 16, line 5, for untellable read unspeakable

The cat by the cellar window is a cat-shaped
absence, in black. The cellar window's a strip-light
at its feet, a chink: the earth opening up.
The air is sticky as ink.

Page 20, line 10, for supplicate read deny
Page 20, line 12, for deny read supplicate

Suppose the man in the cellar looked up,
he'd only see dark behind the darker spikes
of lavender and rosemary. (The cat is quite invisible.)
And he doesn't look up. He is exchanging words
painstakingly. Dust and ink lodge indelibly
in his thumb; it ghosts to its negative, a thumbprint.

He will leave his mark. He works in the half-dark
almost all night. Letter by letter, he is setting things right.

Page 22, line 3, for unspeakable read unjustifiable

He is locking up, he is getting a grip on this story
(the press with its oil-black rollers is waiting),
taking the lead weight of it between two hands,
tilting its lead-black against the ink-black
of the window; taking the first, fresh, impression.

Page 38, line 4, for simulate read assimilate
Page 40, line 2, for clarify read uncurtain

The first principle of design is leaving things out,
is in the spacing and the margins. Seven years
is the time-span for a complete change of skin.

Page 53, line 9, for past read future
Page 54, line 5, for amend read alter
Page 58, line 2, for alter read correct
Page 61, line 6, for correct read impose

The lines are unjustified. The errors are spawning.

Page 61, line 8, for impose read query
Page 62, line 5, the bracket should be closed
after the evidence, *not after* as clearly.

The chase frames the story.
Time and place are composed.

In the room above, a cat tests the floorboards.
It is six o'clock. It is almost morning.
Street-lights turn yellow, the sky comes adrift.
Clouds scud loose and dirt as newsprint.
The house will wake soon. Soon things will happen:
words will be exchanged: irrevocable, unredeemable,
demanding another night's work, and another, over-writing.

Page 70, line 2 for unjustifiable read unrevisable

There are not enough spaces between the days.